ACPL ITEM
DISCARDED
S0-DSF-742

2-9-76

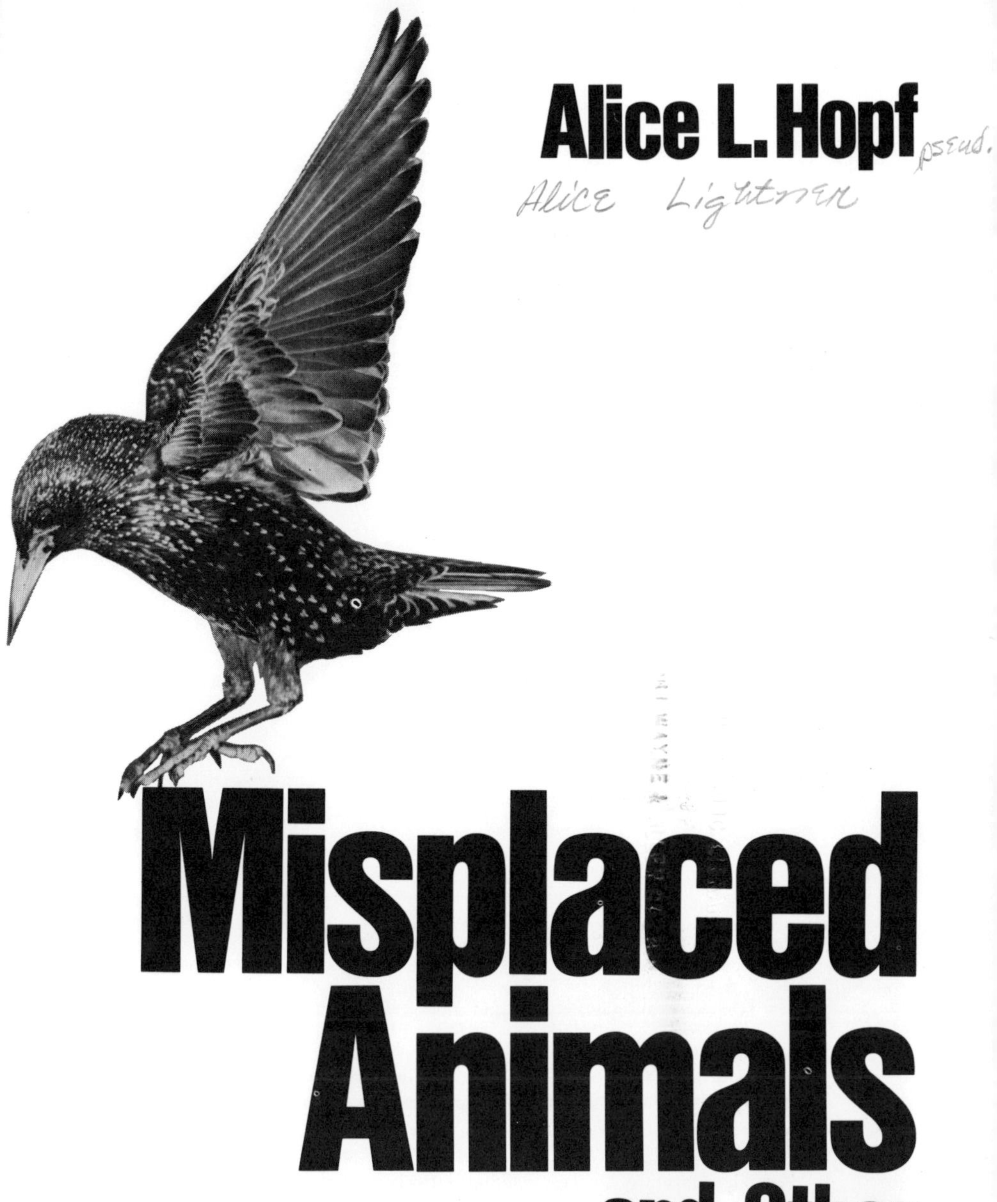

Alice L. Hopf

Misplaced Animals and Other Living Creatures

Illustrated with photographs and drawings

McGraw-Hill Book Company
New York St. Louis San Francisco London Montreal Toronto

Library of Congress Cataloging in Publication Data

Hopf, Alice Lightner,
Misplaced animals, plants, and other creatures.

Includes index.
SUMMARY: Explores the ways in which man and nature have used water, wind, weather, and wings to spread plants and animals around the world with good and bad results.
1. Animal introduction—Juvenile literature. 2. Plant introduction—Juvenile literature. [1. Animal introduction. 2. Plant introduction] I. Title.
QL86.H66 574.5′2 75-10952
ISBN 0-07-030318-5 lib. bdg.

1234567 BPBP 7898765

Contents

Picture appearing on page 100
Courtesy of the **Australian Information Service**

Pictures appearing on pages 31, 48, 78
Courtesy of the **Fish & Wildlife Service**

Pictures appearing on pages 8, 9
Courtesy of **Sturla Fridriksson**

Pictures appearing on pages 4, 55
Courtesy of **Brian Hawkes**

Drawing on page 94
Courtesy of **Freidrich E. Zeuner, HISTORY OF DOMESTICATED ANIMALS, Harper & Row, 1963**

Pictures appearing on pages 85, 87, 89, 92
Courtesy of **Frances Lightner**

Pictures appearing on pages 50, 66, 70, 112, 119, 121, 125
Courtesy of the **National Audubon Society: Karl H. Maslowski, Lynwood M. Chace, William Allen Jr., Treat Davidson, E. C. Higgins, Charlie Ott**

Picture appearing on page 114
Courtesy of the **National Oceanic and Atmospheric Administration**

Pictures appearing on pages 16, 19, 73, 75, 81, 97
Courtesy of **L. Hugh Newman's Natural History Photographic Agency, Kent, England**

Picture appearing on page 22
Courtesy of **Donald W. Nusbaum**

Pictures appearing on pages 58, 60
Courtesy of **Walter Rothenbuhler**

Pictures appearing on pages 27, 107, 110
Courtesy of **Leonard Lee Rue III**

Pictures appearing on pages 41, 43, 45
Courtesy of the **U.S. Department of Agriculture: Larry Rȧna, Murray Lemmon**

For
Claudia
Carroll
Marian
and Karl

I

NATURE'S WAY

1

A New Land

"The time has come," the Walrus said,
"To talk of many things:
Of shoes—and ships—and sealing-wax—
Of cabbages—and kings—
And why the sea is boiling hot—
And whether pigs have wings."

Of all the impossibles in this famous nonsense rhyme, from Lewis Carroll's *Through The Looking-Glass*, perhaps the most impossible is that the sea should be boiling hot. And yet there are times when this does occur, and strangely enough, one place is in the cold north Atlantic off Iceland.

Ancient folk tales and legends describe the miracle of a burning sea, and St. Brendan's story of sailing past the mouth of Hell can be nothing more than the description of a submarine eruption. These eruptions often produce new islands, which in most cases are later engulfed by the sea.

In 1783, such an eruption was observed by a ship's captain, Jörgen Mindelberg, who wrote in his report, "At three o'clock in the morning we saw smoke rising from the sea . . . we concluded that this was a special wonder wrought by God and that a natural sea could burn." And he added, "When I caught sight of this terrifying smoke, I felt convinced that Doomsday had come."

This occurred in the month of May, and when Mindelberg returned to Denmark with his report of the eruption and the island which had been created by it, the Danish government decided to send an expedition there to claim the new land for Denmark. They planned to raise the Danish flag over the island and erect a large stone, carved with the royal insignia. But these things were never done, for when the ship arrived at the site in the following autumn, the island could not be found. Like so many of these volcanic islands, it had sunk once more beneath the sea.

However, occasionally an undersea volcano erupts long enough and strongly enough so that it builds its cone high above the reaching waves and eventually creates a stable and enduring island. This is completely new land, devoid of life of any sort. Yet it is remarkable how quickly life of many kinds manages to find a foothold there and to grow and prosper.

Eruption at Surtsey Island

Such an island is Surtsey, which was born on November 14, 1963, when a great undersea eruption began about four miles west of Geirfuglasker, the southernmost island off the coast of Iceland. This eruption proved to be the second longest in the history of Iceland—a land dotted with volcanoes. It lasted for three and a half years, with many variations and changes, and in the process two other, smaller islands were born and later worn away. The history of the first few years of this island is vividly described by the noted Icelandic geologist, Sigurdur Thorarinsson, in his book, *Surtsey.*

Such undersea eruptions usually begin with fissures that open in the ocean floor. As the seawater rushes in, steam is generated which rises to the surface and gives the impression that the sea is smoking. As the eruption continues, a mountain is created which eventually rises above the water, and an island is born. As more and more material is spewed out, the island becomes larger and the mouth of the volcano is raised farther above the sea. But as long as the sea can get into the volcano, the eruption will be what the geologists call a tephra eruption. Great columns of smoke and fire climb skyward and masses of burning rock are thrown out, which explode like bombs. A blanket of cinders and ash may rain down upon the sea and on any ship that ventures too close, while lightning flashes from the clouds that pile above the newborn island. All the forces of nature seem to be at war, and indeed the sea and the volcano are locked in a titanic struggle. It is only when the earth-building forces have shut out the sea completely from the subterranean fires that a new kind of eruption begins and that the life of the island seems to be assured. For once seawater is kept out, the volcano can create lava. And the lava, rolling down the sides of the young mountain and cutting its burning path to the sea, builds rock that the sea cannot easily wear away.

The lava flow began on Surtsey on April 4, 1964, and continued off and on, building up the island's defenses. This type of eruption is just as spectacular as the explosive kind, and people came in ships and in airplanes to view the fiery rivers flowing to the sea, where they disappeared in clouds of steam and smoke. In fact, there was so much interest in nature's fireworks exhibition that the Icelandic government, urged on by interested scientists, declared the island a sanctuary. This was done in May of 1965. Visitors to the island are now restricted to scientists and to people who are making a serious study of how life comes to and develops on a new land.

The first landing on Surtsey was made in the early days by three French adventurers, sponsored by a Parisian publication. When there seemed to be a lull in the eruption on December 6, 1964, they rushed out in a speedboat from the nearest Icelandic settlement. But they stayed for only a quarter of an hour before the eruption resumed and they thought best to leave.

On February 19 of the following year, Thorarinsson made an expedition to the island with six other scientists, including two women. They approached in a motorboat which stood offshore, while the party went ashore in two rubber dinghies. One of these promptly capsized so that the adventurers were well soaked on arrival. They landed on a sandy beach on the northeastern side and began to explore the new land.

Soon they found a bubbling crater near their point of landing and hoped that it would not impede their work. But they had hardly been ashore more than a few minutes, when the volcano itself began to erupt. Tephra bombs came crashing down around them and they could see waterspouts out to sea. The boat that had brought them was forced to retreat farther from the island, which seemed, to the dismay of those aboard, to disappear in the smoke and clouds.

The scientists had no choice but to wait out the eruption. This involved the exercise of dodging tephra bombs. The geologist says that it is easier than you might think, but that you must stand still and watch the air above you and resist the impulse to run until a bomb seems about to land on your head! After an hour and a half, the tephra showers abated and the group was able to launch their dinghies and reach the safety of their ship. Fortunately, nobody was hurt on this expedition, and no more efforts were made to land on the island until the explosive phase of the eruption was passed.

It is astonishing how quickly life takes advantage of any

new land. In May of 1964, only a month after the lava flow had begun, a biologist found a number of microbes hovering in the air over the island. And later that summer, both butterflies and flies were seen there.

By 1967, 63 species of land invertebrates (insects and such) were listed in the reports. These included flies, wasps, beetles and moths. Also ticks, spiders and one bird louse. By 1970, the list had grown to 136! It included a Painted Lady—the most widely distributed of all butterflies—which was found dead, but "no doubt arrived alive." Most of this growing list of insects and related species were casual visitors, blown to the island or washed ashore with no hope of setting up a permanent colony. None of the flies observed in 1964 had been able to reproduce and survive, but by the summer of 1970, one species of springtail (*collembola*) had become a resident of the Surtsey beach and one species of midge had begun breeding in rock pools.

Of course, the birds were quick to find this new haven in the vast expanse of ocean. Surtsey had been in existence for only two weeks when it was noticed that gulls were alighting there between the explosions. Some observers suggested that perhaps they liked to warm their feet!

Other birds came, too. Thorarinsson lists such species as dunlins, oyster catchers, red-necked phalaropes, ringed plovers, wheatears, snow buntings and kittiwakes. He also mentions the sad case of some guillemots seen wandering on this barren shore. They were oil-soaked birds that had been caught in the refuse from fishing vessels and they had come ashore here to die. In 1965, a pair of ravens made the island their headquarters. As spring approached, they searched the land for nesting sites, but finally gave up the struggle and flew away.

It was not until 1970 that the first birds nested on Surtsey. Kittiwakes and fulmars had been occupying the western cliffs for several summers and in that year there was great excitement among the scientists when the first pair of fulmars built a nest and raised one young. This year also, a pair of black guillemots nested, raising two babies. The observers expected that the kittiwakes would follow suit the next year.

These birds that were building homes on the island were all seabirds, species that could live by fishing. However, the two ravens still came to Surtsey, picking up a living around the beaches, and it was hoped that they might eventually nest also. Many other birds came to the island for a brief stay, especially during migration seasons, when whole flocks would pass over and some individuals stop to rest. In 1967, fourteen species were counted, including such birds as plovers, geese, redwings and a long-eared owl. By 1970, the number had increased to nineteen species per season.

As for plant life, the geologist lists sea rocket (a low plant of the mustard family, with light purple flowers) and lyme grass (wild rye) as the first plants whose seeds drifted ashore. Whole plants sometimes drifted over from the nearest islands, and in 1965, a sea rocket was recorded as the first green plant to have struck roots on Surtsey. This plant grows on the beaches of southern Iceland, but it is believed to have originated in America, whence the seeds were carried by ocean currents.

These first plants had a hard fight for survival. They usually took root where drifted seaweed formed a shelter from sandstorms. But they still had the volcano to contend with,

Lyme grass on Surtsey

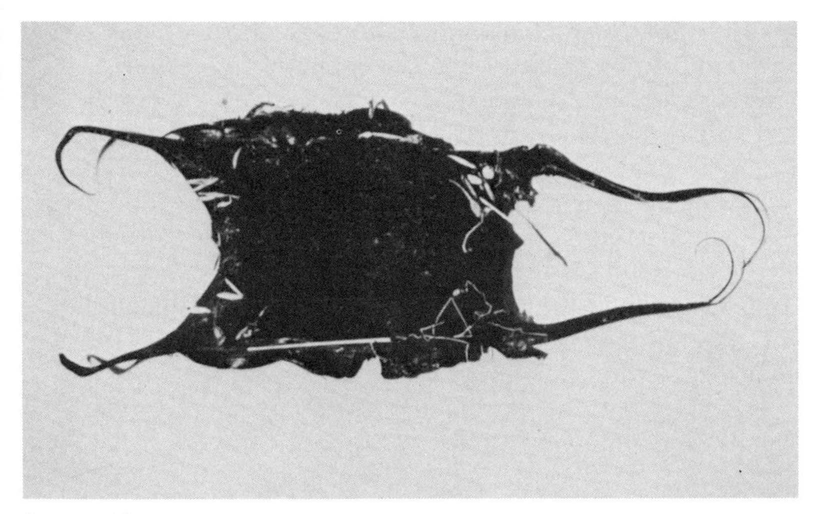

A mermaid purse

and when later eruptions occurred, building up the smaller islands, these plants were often covered with tephra ash. Still, in 1967, the scientists found these hardy plants still growing and that spring for the first time they saw little white flowers blooming amid the volcanic desolation.

In 1969, 63 individual plants of four different species were found on the island, and by 1970 the number had increased to 101 plants, again of four species. In addition to the sea rocket, wild rye, scurvy grass, chickweed and bluebell were discovered. Now some of the plants were getting strong enough to survive the winter. A number of them flowered and even produced seeds. Mosses also arrived, but the scientists suspected that they themselves had brought this growth in on their shoes. Mosses grew best in locations where heat and steam were coming from the island's internal fires.

How did these colonizing plants manage to reach the new island? In many cases, the scientists believe, the seeds drifted onto the beach from the nearest islands or from Iceland itself. But other methods have been noted. Some surprise seed carriers, washed up on the Surtsey beaches, were those curiosities of the sea known as mermaid's purses. These are the egg cases of one of the skates and have a rough, shell-like covering to which the seeds had stuck. Most of the seeds turned out to be those of grasses common to Iceland.

Of course, birds are some of the greatest dispersers of seeds, and this was proved when plants were found growing around a barrel that had been left on the island to collect rainwater. Birds had found this a welcome innovation, and as they perched on the rim to drink, their droppings had fallen to the ground outside the barrel. Not only did these droppings contain seeds that the birds had eaten in some distant land, but they provided the only soil and nourishment for the sprouting seed in this land of rock and lava.

Various forms of marine life soon appeared around the island. Sometimes the sands were pink with tiny shrimplike creatures, a boon to the oyster catchers. At other times the scientists found varicolored cuttlefish washed up on the black sands. One such, till then unknown to Iceland, was identified as a native of the Caribbean.

Seals showed an interest in the island from the very beginning, but not until the explosive tephra eruptions had abated did they go ashore. Then they could often be found sunning themselves and sleeping on the beach. Since Surtsey has been declared a sanctuary, the seals are safe there from harassment by men, and they seem to sense that fact. Indeed, one time Thorarinsson found a young harbor seal lying next to a young professor—both of them sound asleep!

One thing that impressed Dr. Thorarinsson was the speed with which the landscape on Surtsey changed. All his training in his profession had conditioned him to expect slow changes in the earth. Modern geology teaches that the earth was built by slight changes occurring over the millennia, the gradual wearing away of rock by wind and water, as can be seen in the strata of the cliffs of the Grand Canyon. There each layer of rock represents thousands—even tens of thousands—of years. But here before his eyes, Thorarinsson saw the face of the earth altered in a matter of days.

In a few months a completely new land was created with an unbelievably varied landscape. There was a lava dome with a lava lake in the crater from which lava streams rushed down to the sea, changing the shape of the island from day to day. There were gravel banks and sandy beaches, and great white cliffs towering above lagoons. Around all this the sea and the volcano battled constantly. One day you might find a beach covered with flowing lava, steaming as it met the sea. A few weeks later, at the same spot, you would find high lava cliffs and below them boulders, already worn by the sea to a smooth roundness. The opposite forces of building and eroding worked so fast that the landscape seemed to change daily before the eyes of the fascinated scientists.

There has been some controversy among scientists about the earth-building forces that have shaped our world. It is now believed that the volcanic forces active along the Atlantic Ridge, which created Surtsey in a few weeks, are also involved in slow movements on the ocean floor which result in the continents moving apart.

The theory of continental drift has only been widely accepted in this century. And strangely, it was the study of animal life that clinched the matter. The finding of ancient dinosaur fossils on Antarctica, similar to those found in India, has proved that the two continents must once have been close together.

Another animal mystery, which may be clarified by continental drift, is the problem of the green sea turtles. These large turtles annually make a 1,200-mile swim from South America to Ascension Island in the Atlantic, where they lay their eggs. How do they know where they are going? How do they navigate to an island far beyond sight and smell?

Turtles are a very old form of life, and it seems likely that there were green turtles living in the coastal waters of Brazil when that land was still in close proximity to Africa. At that time, it was only a short swim for the turtles to an island they could see and that offered a safe place to lay their eggs. As South America drifted slowly to the west, the distance to the island lengthened. But the increase in distance was not apparent to any individual turtle. Generations of these animals hatched and made the swim back and forth without noticing that the journey was gradually getting longer.

This is something of a simplification of what the scientists believe took place. Dr. Archie Carr, well-known herpetologist and Patrick J. Coleman, an Australian geophysicist, worked together on the theory, which assumes not just one island—

the one we now know as Ascension—but a series of volcanic islands.

The scientists believe that 80 million years ago, when South America was still close to Africa, the turtles, whose fossils are still found from that period, had only a short swim from their grazing waters along what is now the coast of Brazil to the island where they laid their eggs. But as the continents moved inexorably apart and the sea floor sank, the island would sink, too. However, new islands would be formed by the same volcanic forces that have just now built the island of Surtsey. As the sea floor continued to widen, pushing the continents apart, the islands would also move westward, becoming submerged one by one, while a new island was built up behind them. These submerged islands, which are really the tops of undersea mountains, are known as seamounts. When soundings were made of the ocean floor between Brazil and Ascension Island, they did indeed find a string of over a dozen seamounts. Each one of these, in its time above water, may have been a nesting haven for the green turtles.

Dr. Carr points out that this turtle has great shoulder muscles and has developed the habit of storing up fat for its journey. Both these characteristics must have been developed over the millennia as one generation of turtles after another made an ever-lengthening swim back and forth from their grazing waters to their breeding islands.

The shifts and changes of our physical world have their influence on the creatures that live in it. The entire population of an island may be wiped out by a tidal flood or a volcanic eruption. But new life will creep back, some quickly and some slowly. All of it will adjust to the situation and a stable environment will develop.

But a new factor has been added in the last few thousand years. Man has spread throughout the world, and we have taken other forms of life with us. We have brought plants and animals and birds to every new land that we have settled. Some of this life came along with us without being asked, and often by accident. But much of it was brought on purpose, and most of these willful importations did not work out in quite the happy way that the importers had expected.

II

LONG-TIME FOLLOWERS

2

The Ubiquitous Pigeon

The pigeon (*Columba livia*) is found today on all continents and in all the big cities of the world. In fact, everywhere except the polar regions. But they are native to few of these places. As people moved across the oceans and filled up the good living places of the earth, they took pigeons with them. Many of these birds escaped from their half-domestic status and became feral—that is, they went back to the wild. But they found living around people so much to their liking that they went right on doing so. This is why we now have flocks of millions of pigeons living in our big cities. Recently, it was estimated that there are around five million pigeons in the streets of New York City.

Many people like to watch the aerial acrobatics of these birds as they wheel and soar in unison about the city parks and squares. Some people go out of their way to feed them. But in recent years the pigeon has come to be regarded as something of a pest. In fact, a dangerous pest. A million birds can make a lot of excrement. It piles up in air shafts and below ledges where the birds roost. It dirties the statues and the

Feeding pigeons, Trafalgar Square

benches in the parks. Aside from the occasional irate citizen who has gotten pigeon droppings in her hair or on his clothes, there is the problem of the masonry and the sculptures that enhance many of our great cities. It has been found that these are gradually being eroded and are falling into decay because of the tons of pigeon dung, which combined with the industrial air pollution of the big cities, has a corrosive effect. Besides New York City, complaints come from such art centers as Venice and Paris, London and Rome, where priceless art from the past ages is being irreparably destroyed.

But the threat of city pigeons does not end there. They have been found to be a serious health hazard. Everyone knows that city air is contaminated by industrial fumes. But now it seems that pigeon dung gets blown around and adds to the contamination. The dust from such dung carries a fungus, which, when inhaled, enters the lungs and causes a disease called *cryptococcosis*. The symptoms may be like those of a bad cold, or even appear to be bronchitis or tuberculosis. The fungus can also cause a form of meningitis (brain fever) which until some ten years ago was always fatal. An antifungal drug has now cut the death rate down to around 30 percent. Pigeons also carry other diseases, such as *psittacosis* (parrot fever).

With all these marks against it, there is little wonder that recent years have seen a demand for the extermination of the city pigeon. But this is easier said than done. Pigeon executioners face the wrath of pigeon lovers, and city officials have had to resort to surreptitious shooting or trapping of the birds in the early hours when few people are about on the streets. Many other methods have been tried of scaring the birds away, most of them unsuccessful. Cities have installed electrified grids, supersonic whistles and cat and snake dummies. Perhaps the most successful is a gooey chemical that can be painted on building ledges and which gives the birds both a hotfoot and produces a repellent odor. Some cities have tried feeding birth control drugs to the birds. But the most effective method is simply to stop feeding them, and many cities have passed laws against this pastime. But human nature being what it is, the ban is seldom enforced and the pigeons in their millions are still with us.

Pigeons were not always so widely spread around the world. Their original homeland was in the mountainous regions of Europe and Asia. They needed two things in order to survive: steep, inaccessible cliffs where their eggs could be safe from predators, and green valleys nearby, with plenty of food and water within easy flying distance.

Both these things were available in the hills of Mesopotamia, a region now covered by the countries of Iran and Iraq. And it was here that man first developed the art of farming, using the wild grains that grew on those same hills. Little by little, the farms grew into villages and the villages grew into cities. And the pigeons, coming down from their nesting ledges every day in search of food, found that the growing farms were a great bonanza.

Before long, the pigeons found it easier to build their nests in the eaves of the new houses and barns. And as the towns grew into cities, and bigger buildings were built, the pigeons selected the tallest as their nesting places. In these early cities, the biggest buildings were the temples, with tall pillars and decorated stone work, all supplying ledges reminiscent of the pigeons' ancient homes.

Thus the pigeons became temple birds and as such were considered sacred. Oracles were told on the way the birds flew. Or if the bird was sacrificed to the god, its entrails were consulted by the priests as a way of foretelling the future. In the Hebrew religion, and later in the Christian, the pigeon was considered a bird of peace and love. It was a pigeon that Noah released from the Ark to find land when the Flood was subsiding.

However, even though the pigeon was a sacred bird, that did not prevent it from being eaten. Soon after the birds began to live in close proximity with man, they must have been used as food. They are the easiest domestic bird to care for. A handful of extra grain thrown out occasionally, and the farmer has a source of food ready at hand. Exactly when the situation changed from encouragement of a wild bird to the rearing of a domestic one, is not known. But people were dining off pigeons as far back as 4500 B.C., for their bones are found in excavations and they appear in the early terracotta art from Mesopotamia. Even before the Mycenaean Period (1400 to 1100 B.C.) they were being raised in dovecotes.

This method of rearing pigeons, known as dovecote culture, is very ancient. A stone tower was built, with nesting holes and ledges for the pigeons. It was arranged for easy access to the nests, so that eggs and young birds (squabs) could be taken for food. The pigeons remained in a wild state, feeding themselves, perhaps with some help from the owner. This method is believed to have originated in Asia, or possibly with the Etruscans. Soon it had spread all over the ancient world, and was perfected by the Romans. Hardly a "Roman banquet" without pigeon or squab on the menu!

City pigeons

The Romans introduced the pigeon to all the lands that they conquered and are responsible for its arrival in Britain. Dovecote culture continued after the fall of Rome and throughout the Middle Ages. It is still in use in some parts of the world today. During the Middle Ages, the dovecote was part of the lord's castle. The peasants had to pay a yearly tithe of what they grew to the castle. But they also had to allow the lord's pigeons to forage unmolested among their crops. So that in reality they paid a double tax, and many a poor farmer prayed in church for relief from the lord's pigeons.

Just when people discovered the pigeon's remarkable homing instinct is another matter in dispute. But it is certain that it was being put to good use early in the Ancient World. It is recorded that when Ramses III was crowned in 1198 B.C. in Egypt, four pigeons were dispatched to the four directions, announcing the accession of the new ruler. And by the fifth century B.C., the use of carrier pigeons was well known by the Greeks, who used them to bring word of martial victories and for other political and commercial messages.

The Romans adopted the system from the Greeks, and news of Caesar's victories in Gaul were sent to Rome by carrier pigeon. Some centuries later, Nero was using such pigeons to carry news of the day's circus contests from Rome to friends in the country.

Messenger pigeons seem to have fallen into disuse during the Dark Ages in Europe. But the practice was developed to a high degree by the Arabs. A sultan in Baghdad is said to have set up the first pigeon mail, around A.D. 1150, and the Mamelukes in Egypt bred special pigeons for this purpose, keeping careful records in studbooks. Later this art was introduced into Europe through the Crusaders and by the Arabs in Spain. Pigeons are still revered in many of the Mohammedan countries. And in Bombay, India, as recently as 1925, there was a near riot when some European boys killed a few street pigeons.

The first use of pigeons by an army is believed to have been made by Genghis Khan. Even to the present day, armies have found them useful in keeping open communications. At the siege of Paris, in 1870, they were the only means of sending word into the beleaguered city from the forces outside. In World War I, when radio was still in its infancy, they were used extensively along the front, where telephone and telegraph communications often broke down. At the end of the war, decorations were handed out to pigeons that had flown bravely through shellfire to deliver their messages. They were still being used during World War II and only recently did the Army Signal Corps dismantle its pigeon lofts. These birds have served the country well, some flying over 1,000 miles to reach their destinations. The record set by a Signal Corps bird was 2,300 miles.

Even ten years ago, carrier pigeons were being used in Japan. That country is so used to suffering devastation by earthquakes, when all modern communication systems may be destroyed, that pigeons bring a welcome insurance. Several of their big newspapers have maintained pigeon lofts on their roofs and use the birds for special news coups. Thus, when U.S. Secretary of the Interior, Stewart Udall, climbed Mount Fuji in 1961, a news photographer took a pigeon along and dispatched it homeward with a photographic film which appeared on the front page of the paper's special edition.

With their avid interest in sports, it seems odd that the Romans never took carrier pigeons one step further and developed racing. But it was not until fairly recent times (1815 is the earliest date given) that pigeon racing began. It was first developed in Belgium and somewhat later (1871) the English took it up. From there it spread to America. Today the racing of pigeons is almost a worldwide sport.

Each country has developed its own breeds of racing pigeons. And it is when this kind of careful crossbreeding is done to bring out a certain desired characteristic, that an animal can be said to be really domesticated. In the dovecote culture, pigeons remained wild to a great extent. They were allowed to fly as they pleased and to mate as the fancy took them. They foraged for food on their own.

But when pigeons were used as messengers, they were confined to their lofts and only allowed to fly free when carrying messages. Great care was taken about crossbreeding so as to develop stronger and faster flyers. Like the Arabs, who hundreds of years ago were keeping studbooks on their pigeons, today's pigeon fanciers keep careful records of their pigeons' pedigrees.

Breeders give all sorts of fancy names to their breeds as well as to individual pigeons. The Smerle, the Cumulet, the Dragoon, the Flying Horseman, and the Carrier are just a few of the early breeds. The first breeders had concentrated on such aspects as color and arrangements of feathers. They had produced such birds as the pouter, the tumbler and the fantail. But when breeding began for good racing stock, such considerations were discarded. Color no longer mattered, but speed, endurance and homing ability did.

British and American racing did not get started till after the Franco-Prussian War. Perhaps the fact that dovecote culture had for centuries been entirely in the hands of the nobility discouraged the average Englishman from looking kindly upon pigeons. Then later the use of carrier pigeons by the embattled Parisians may have stirred the imagination. Moreover, training the birds in the early days was difficult. Transporting them the required distance from home was a slow and expensive job.

However, it did not take the British and Americans long to catch up with the pigeon racers of the Continent, and by 1878 a prize of $100 was being offered for the first bird to fly 500

Start of a pigeon race

miles. Shortly after this, the Army Signal Corps added impetus to the breeding of racers by taking up their use for distant stations in the West and in Indian warfare. By 1896, 500 miles flown in one day had become commonplace, and with improved breeding of birds, those records have long since been broken. By 1920, a hen pigeon, called Smoky Girl, had won the 500-mile trophy three times in succession, and a male called Sparkler flew 619 miles on "day of toss"—two years in succession.

Today different sections of the country have their own racing meets in which various clubs take part. The Midwest Classic, held in Topeka, Kansas, in June of 1974, brought 6,000 pigeons together from 500 lofts in 11 states. The pigeons had to fly up to 500 miles. The birds are taken to the starting point in a truck that opens in such a way that they all fly out at once. The flight distance to each loft has been carefully measured by an air survey firm so that the bird's speed can later be computed from the exact second when it arrives home. Special timers are used to prevent cheating by overenthusiastic fanciers.

Pigeons are banded in much the same way that migratory

birds are banded, and the numbers, along with the names and addresses of owners, are published in the annual bulletin of the American Racing Pigeon Union. Thus, a lost pigeon, found far from home, can be easily returned to its loft. Not all homers are infallible and they often get into difficulties along the way. In fact, some of them never return at all, falling victim to such hazards of the flyways as hawks and eagles, or lured to another loft by a member of the opposite sex. Sometimes they hit power lines, which are strung at the pigeon's flying height. Once a bird gets lost, it is scratched from racing, for its confidence has been undermined. This was the fate of one unfortunate pigeon, tossed outside Los Angeles, with only a twenty-five-mile flight to its home. It was found eventually perched in a tree beside the Panama Canal! Other ill-fated birds have been known to fly low over oil sumps, looking for a drink of water, only to get their feathers soaked with oil. And in 1971, some 20,000 homing pigeons got lost in a British fog, although most of them reached home when the fog lifted.

Pigeons usually fly at about 50 mph. in these races. One racer from Milwaukee, Wisconsin averaged 76 mph. in a 100-mile race. Though of course, just as in horse racing and dog racing, owners have their little tricks for getting the best time out of a bird. One such ruse is to take a setting hen pigeon and switch her eggs, so that she unexpectedly finds that her clutch is about to hatch. Then she is taken off the nest and shipped to the starting point of the race. Naturally, she will bend every wing feather to get back to her brood as soon as possible.

Like everything else, the cost of keeping a loft of racing pigeons has risen over the years. One owner states that he spends $1,000 a year on his pigeons. Good birds can bring from $200 to $500 apiece, and a champion racer in England, named Workman, was recently bought for $10,000. But the prize money and bets have risen also, and thousands of dollars may change hands at a meet..

Pigeons are prolific birds, one reason they so quickly become pests. Although they lay only two eggs at a time in a nest made of a few sticks scraped together, the eggs hatch in eighteen days. In another month the young birds are almost ready to fly. So pigeons can raise several broods in a year. This is facilitated by the fact that the male as well as the female takes part in raising the young. Baby birds are fed a diet of "pigeon milk," which is digested food from the crops of both the parents. It looks a bit like curdled milk and is regurgitated for the babies until they are a week old. After the first week, it comes mixed with half-digested grain, until the young are able to eat whole grains. Since the male pigeon is capable of feeding the babies by himself, the female often starts incubating another nest of eggs.

Thus the feral pigeon populations of our cities are able to expand their numbers indefinitely. And as we build taller and taller skyscrapers, we provide more and better nesting ledges for the birds. The pigeon has followed us a long way from the temples of Mesopotamia and the ages of prehistory. We are still providing them with food and lodging to fit their original needs, even though our need for them has greatly diminished and they are now more of a pest than a pet. We are told that the one sure way to get rid of them is to stop feeding them. But from past performance, it seems that it may be a long time before that happens.

3

The Unbeatable Rat

The rat is another creature that has made its way around the world, assisted by the cooperation of humans. It has not been with us a fraction of the time that the pigeon has been, and it does not bring with it any of the advantages of that bird. In fact, the rat has been a downright danger and disadvantage for the entire time that we have known it. But like the pigeon, we seem incapable of ridding ourselves of this pest.

There are many species of wild rats around the world. Pack rats, kangaroo rats, water rats, banana rats, to list only a few. But these various species of rats tend to stay where they belong—in the wild. Not so the big brown and black rats, which have become accustomed to living in and around the homes of people, and which over the years have used our ships and vehicles to spread all over the world.

Rats seem to have been unknown in the Ancient World. And although the bones of rats have been found in excavations of early man, such as the lake dwellers of Switzerland, there is no way of knowing if the animals were being used for food or if they had already developed the habit of being hangers-on of *Homo sapiens*. The learned men of ancient Greece and Rome, who studied and described the animals that populated their world, made occasional mention of mice, but said not a word about rats.

There are two distinct species of house rats, popularly known as the black rat and the brown rat. But as both species vary in shadings of black and brown, this is not a very good identification. The black rat arrived on the scene first. Its scientific name is *Rattus rattus* and it is believed to have come from the Arabian desert. At some point it discovered that life was easier around the tents and camps of men than scrounging for food in the wilderness. By the twelfth century, the time of the Crusades, they were well settled in the Arab cities, and when the Christian expeditions returned from the Holy Land, *Rattus rattus* came along in their ships. Ever since that time, rats have been very fond of ships. People eventually learned how to put rat-guards on the hawsers that tied the ships to shore. But sailors sometimes forget to put up the guards, and either way, rats are ingenious creatures and they manage to get aboard by one means or another. Even today, it is hard to keep a ship rat-free. And in this way, more than any other, rats have spread across the oceans and around the world.

Rattus rattus is the smaller of the two species. It is slender with a long tail and can climb and jump gracefully. It is also known as the Alexandrine rat, because of its connection with the East, and the roof rat, because of its ability to nest in the eaves of roofs. In color it ranges from black to tawny, with a pale underbelly.

The so-called brown rat has a shorter tail and a shorter nose than its cousin, the black rat. It is not as good a climber, but is an expert burrower and a much fiercer fighter. Where black and brown have come face to face, the brown has always conquered. Because this rat was believed to have come to England in a shipment of timber from Norway, it became known as the Norway rat, and the word has gone into the scientific name, *Rattus norvegicus*.

The Norway rat did not turn up in European cities till some six hundred years after its black cousin. By this time, Europeans were used to rats. The rat catcher had an honored

Brown rat

position in society during the Middle Ages. There were even Rat Catchers Guilds. And in later centuries, much effort was expended on trapping and killing rats. But there was scant diminution in the number of black rats until the brown ones arrived. These quickly drove out and killed off the weaker species. Brown rats did not really come from Norway. They are thought to have come from Asia, some authorities mentioning Mongolia and others the area around the Caspian Sea. Whatever their origin, by the year 1727 they were invading Europe and a few had reached England by 1728.

Both species are now established in America—in fact, pretty much all over the world. They are thought to have arrived here soon after the Revolution. It is the brown rat that has taken over our cities and farm lands. The black rat is more numerous in seaports and in the tropics, where the brown is at a disadvantage, being a less agile climber.

The amount of destruction a rat can do is almost endless. The most important is contamination of foodstuffs. One reason the rat is so successful as a species is that it will eat anything. Anything we will eat—and a lot more. And what they eat is only a small part of the food they damage. A few rats in a storage cellar can result in bags of flour chewed open and the contents spilling out—potatoes, apples, carrots, with only a bite taken from each. If there are baby chicks in a run, a rat will kill most of them while it can eat only one or two. It has been estimated that India alone harbors 2.4 billion rats, which destroy at least 2.4 million tons of food grains yearly.

In addition to the millions of dollars that rats cost us in food damage each year, they can also cause huge losses by fire and flood. Rats have a peculiar kind of teeth, a specialty of all rodents. Their four front teeth grow so fast that they must be constantly gnawing on something in order to grind them down. Otherwise, the teeth would soon grow into the opposite jaw. Consequently, the rat has a continuous urge to chew on something, and if it isn't food, it might well be wood, a lead pipe, concrete or steel. Rats have gnawed holes in dams and caused floods. They have started fires by carrying matches into their nests. They have blacked out a city by chewing the insulation off wires. And of course, they have been known to bite people, especially children and babies, in the poorer sections of our big cities.

During World War II and the years that followed, intensive studies of the rat were undertaken in England in an effort to halt the destruction of vital food stocks. Some interesting facts about rat psychology came to light in this work. For centuries rats have been credited with having unusual intelligence. They have consistently learned to avoid traps and to detect poisoned bait. But when studied scientifically, it became possible to explain their behavior.

For one thing, rats are intensely curious animals. Placed in a new environment (as was done with the rats being studied and as would be true of rats coming off a ship in a new port), they have a great urge to go exploring. Psychologists investigating the rat's intelligence have found that the opportunity to explore can be used as a "reward" as well as food. In fact, a hungry rat will often explore a new situation before it will eat.

This urge to explore is not limited to the physical surroundings. It is carried over into the rat's eating habits. A rat will nibble at a dozen different food items, if such are available. This is why so much more food is damaged than is actually eaten. It is also why rats are so difficult to exterminate with poison. A rat takes a tiny bite of the poisoned bait and moves on to other investigations. If it then feels sick from the poison, it will carefully avoid all such bait in the future.

To get around this problem, some exterminators have adopted a method called "prebaiting." Samples of unpoisoned bait are left around until the rats become accustomed to them as good food. A bit later, the samples are injected with poison. The rats, having become accustomed to the food, will presumably eat enough of the poison to be killed. Other, more deadly poisons have also been developed, including one that prevents blood from clotting so that the animals soon bleed to death. But care must be taken that valued domestic animals do not get to these poisons.

Rats can live from three to five years, and during that time they are prodigious breeders. They can breed every month of the year and their litters average from six to nine babies. From these facts, it has been estimated that 350 million rats could be produced by a single pair in only three years!

Rats are also credited with an ability to pick the best food for themselves with the highest nutritional value. After sampling and investigating all the food available, they will pick the food most suited to their needs. This has been proved in experiments where the rats were first made salt-deficient and then given a choice of plain or salty water. They invariably chose the salt water. This has also occurred in experiments with some vitamins.

The rat is an animal with a survival ability equal to humans. It is estimated that there are as many rats in the country as there are people—if not more. They adjust to almost any environment or set of conditions. Their curiosity leads them into new lands and at the same time protects them from dangers. They can subsist on almost anything in the way of food.

We do not like to accord the word *intelligence* to any species besides ourselves. But the rat has a lot of something very close to intelligence. Part of this is a good memory. If it eats one little nibble of something unpleasant, it will remember and avoid it in the future. Laboratory white rats have been given intelligence tests and come out very well. In one case, they showed an ability to pick out a certain magazine advertisement for ice cream from a number of other ads. And testers have found that they often make a better score when given five choices than when given two. This has been interpreted as being due to boredom (a very human quality). The rats become bored with the simple test and stop trying!

Rat behavior has been studied quite thoroughly in the period since the Second World War. Rats, of course, are social and gregarious animals. They can live in crowded conditions and like to sleep huddled close together. In one experiment, twelve male rats were put into a cage. None of them knew any of the others, yet they settled down to a friendly existence together. This appeared unusual because six of them were *R. rattus* and six were *R. norvegicus,* and it is well known that the two species fight violently when they meet in the wild.

In another experiment, six males and six females were caged together, all Norway rats. Within a few weeks, all males but the largest were dead. The females remained in good condition. This was interesting to the scientists, for although it is very hard for people to get rid of rats, the animals do kill each other off under certain circumstances.

One such situation is when a strange male rat enters the territory of a rat colony. He will be slaughtered in a very short time. This does not seem to apply to female rats, which are seldom attacked, or to the young, which are never harmed. How do rats recognize a stranger? It is thought that rats living together must acquire a group smell which distinguishes them from any outsider that may try to join them.

Like all animals living in groups, rats have certain social signals by which they organize their behavior. One such is for a rat to crawl underneath another rat. This is done especially by males and is usually an effort of one rat to placate another and ward off a fight. Grooming is done as a friendly gesture, one rat nibbling at the fur of another. They also walk over each other, especially in friendly groups.

When rats fight, it is usually the outsider that is defeated, though sometimes it is a case of the weaker male that succumbs to the attack of a stronger. Strangely, these weaker victims do not always die of wounds or of hunger from being kept away from food. Often the dead rat appears to be quite uninjured. This has puzzled observers, and the conclusion reached is that such rats die of shock. This recalls some strange human deaths, referred to by one scientist as "voodoo deaths," in which the victim shows no physical cause and has apparently succumbed to emotional stress.

These remarkable animals that have followed us around the world and lived off our reluctant largesse for centuries are more serious opponents than the often feared tigers and wolves. We measure the toll they take from us in millions of dollars. And yet the matter of their destructiveness is the smaller part of a double threat. For rats are far more deadly in their capacity as carriers of disease. And the worst disaster so far to overwhelm mankind and threaten our extinction was brought about by the rat.

Today, with our wonder drugs and the belief that science and technology can solve almost anything, it is hard to grasp the extent of the panic that bubonic plague, or the Black Death, evoked during the Middle Ages. In only three years—

Norway rat and nest

between 1348 and 1350—this disease killed a quarter of the population of Europe! There was no cure for it and no escape. Nobody knew the cause, for the microscope had not yet been invented nor the germ theory of disease developed. It was generally believed to be a punishment from God, visited upon people because of their sins.

The terrorized citizens fled from towns and cities by the thousands, and in so doing spread the disease to the country. Lawlessness and immorality were everywhere, people seeming to believe that if they were going to die shortly, they might as well take and enjoy what they could. Others crowded the churches to pray. The rich people shut themselves up in their country houses, hoping to escape infection. Pictures of this behavior have been portrayed in such stories as Boccaccio's *Decameron* and Poe's *Masque of the Red Death.* There was also great cruelty perpetrated, and Jews and witches were burned because they were thought to be responsible. Even doctors were accused, since their efforts to halt the plague failed, and some were stoned in the streets of France. In many places, the countryside went back to wilderness because there was no one left to work the farms. And in 1563, Queen Elizabeth fled London for Windsor Castle, where she had a gallows set up at the gate. Anyone coming there from the city was to be hanged forthwith.

We now know that there are three forms of plague: bubonic, which produces swellings of the lymph glands; pneumonic, which affects the lungs; and septicemic, which poisons the blood. The disease is spread by the bite of a flea, and the fleas are carried by rats. The victims die within two to six days.

Many diseases such as plague are endemic in eastern countries. That is, they appear to be dormant, only a few cases occurring now and then, the bacilli remaining alive in the animal population. Then all at once the disease will become active and spread wildly. The great epidemic of the Black Death began in the seaports of Italy, so probably it was brought by rats from ships coming from the East. In any case, within three years it had spread all over Europe and the death toll was awesome. There were repeated outbreaks recurring about every ten years. In London, there were twenty such during the fifteenth century. And in 1665, there was an epidemic that killed a tenth of London's people.

After that, the plague mysteriously vanished. There have been many attempts to explain the disappearance of plague in Europe, none of them satisfactory. One such theory is that the black rats were killed off by the arrival of the brown rats. But it seems that the plague was subsiding long before the brown rats appeared, and furthermore, the brown rats did not entirely kill off their black relatives.

Bubonic plague is not the only disease that rats can carry. There is a long list of such, including amoebic dysentery, jaundice, rabies and typhus. This last is transmitted from rat to man by lice and has been responsible for many devastating epidemics. Hans Zinsser, in his classic book, *Rats, Lice and History,* shows how typhus has won more battles and wars than the generals and emperors. Wherever men are gathered together in great numbers and close proximity and in poor living conditions, as happens when an army assembles, rats and lice will be prevalent and disease quickly follows. Then the soldiers spread the disease among the towns they conquer and take it back with them to their homes.

Only during World War II was this chain of events broken by the development of DDT. By sprinkling this chemical over the soldiers and their clothing, the armies were sufficiently deloused so that violent epidemics were prevented. But doctors traveling with armies know that they must ever be on guard for the appearance of one disease or another and that only prompt action can prevent an epidemic.

A whole new branch of medical science has developed in modern times which organizes the prevention and control of epidemic diseases. These scientists are constantly on the alert at seaports and airports and it is because of them that we do not have in this country the terrible diseases that are rampant in such places as India, Africa and other tropical countries. However, unceasing vigilance is required. It is known that plague is endemic among the ground squirrels of California. As recently as 1963, a dead rat was found in San Francisco that was infected with bubonic plague. Had it been wandering in the wilds and made contact with a ground squirrel? Nobody knows, but health authorities continue to keep watch.

Perhaps we should ask, what good is a rat? Undoubtedly, the rat was as good as any animal in its original environment. It was part of the balance of nature and had its place in the world food chain. It was only when it became a scavenger in human cities that it became a pest and a carrier of disease and death.

Rats are very helpful to science as laboratory animals. A special strain of white rats has been developed for this purpose. These come originally from albino Norway rats and can breed back with the ordinary domestic rat. They are used for all kinds of experiments, from cancer research to psychological testing. Such white rats also make good pets, sometimes being kept in a cage with an exercise wheel attached, where they can run indefinitely by turning the wheel.

An ironic situation, where it seems to have been better to have the domestic rat than not, has turned up in Western Africa. The story is related in the new book, *Fever,* by John C. Fuller, in which the author describes the work of dedicated scientists in trying to find the source of a mysterious African disease, called Lassa fever. This disease has a habit of appearing and disappearing for no known reason. It is caused by a deadly virus, and scientists have been worried that it might break out and cause a worldwide epidemic.

Almost all the victims of Lassa fever died, and the book details the inspiring story of the courageous work of a few scientists who tried to understand and control this very dangerous disease. When the breakthrough came, after years of devoted labor, it was found that a wild rat, *Mastomys natalensis,* was the animal reservoir of the Lassa fever virus. Most of the time, the huts of the villagers were overrun by black rats, which kept the wild rats out. But now and then the villagers would kill off the rats in their houses and then the wild rats would creep in, bringing with them the virus of Lassa fever. When the villagers got tired of killing rats and the black rats returned to the houses, they chased the wild rats out, and the epidemic subsided.

Today there seems to be small hope of exterminating our

fellow traveler, the rat. The best we can do is to try to control the numbers. But already some rats are becoming immune to our strong poison, warfarin, which is really nothing more than an anticoagulant. It keeps the rat's blood from clotting, so that it bleeds to death. But now "super-rat," genetically resistant, has evolved. It can eat ten times the normal lethal dose without suffering any ill effect.

Civilization as we know it presents a bonanza to the rat. As soon as we humans gave up the simple life of hunting, fishing and gathering, and settled down to permanent homes in farms and towns and cities, the rat, like the pigeon, saw a good thing and moved in.

In our cities, there is always plenty for the rat to eat. There are no predators to speak of to threaten him. Well, a cat or a dog now and then. But the natural predators, such as hawks, eagles, ferrets, weasels, coyotes, are not encouraged in cities. In fact, they are not encouraged within our civilization at all. Even in the wild, where they might keep down the numbers of those menacing ground squirrels, these helpful predators are being destroyed! And so the rat prospers. In spite of poisons and traps, which he is intelligent enough to circumvent most of the time, we have made a good life for him. He will probably be with us for a long time to come.

III

ACCIDENTS WILL HAPPEN

4

The Voracious Caterpillars

About a hundred years ago, in 1869, a French scientist named Trouvelot was living at Medford, Massachusetts. He thought it would be a good thing for the country if a silk industry could be developed here such as flourishes in the Orient and in France. The silkworm is a caterpillar that feeds only on mulberry trees, and Trouvelot thought things would go better if he could develop a worm that would eat a variety of foliage.

With this in mind, M. Trouvelot decided to try to cross the ordinary silkworm with another moth having less specialized tastes. He selected the gypsy moth (*Porthetria dispar*) from Czechoslovakia, and imported both these insects to his home in Medford. The gypsy moth is about the same size as the silkworm moth. In both species the males only can fly, the females being unable to use their wings.

Not much more is known about M. Trouvelot's experiment. Presumably, he was unable to get a fertile cross between the two insects, for no great silk industry has been established here around moths that eat more leaves than the mulberry. Unfortunately, something much more unpleasant occurred. Somehow or other, the imported gypsy moth got loose in the countryside. Just how this happened has not been recorded. Some writers say that they escaped out the window. But this seems unlikely, since the females cannot fly. More probably, when the experiment was finished, the live material was thrown out with the trash. Perhaps the scientist did not realize the danger, or perhaps it was done by a servant, sent to clean up his room.

However it happened, within a few years the citizens of Medford found that they had a new pest in their midst. Caterpillars invaded their shade trees by the thousands, dropping down upon people who sat or passed beneath. What's more, an infestation of these caterpillars could strip the leaves off a tree within a short time, and if the tree was denuded too much or too often, it died.

In Europe, the gypsy moth fits into the ecology of the countryside. There are many natural predators, parasites and diseases which keep its population in check so that it never becomes a pest. Not enough caterpillars survive to destroy the forests. Just enough of them live to keep everything in balance. But in the New World most of these checks do not exist. So when Trouvelot's insects escaped to the wild, they quickly multiplied in number and began to spread through the New England states. Since the female does not fly, they spread slowly. When first out of the egg, the tiny caterpillars hang by a thread of silk and are windblown from tree to tree. This method is slow compared to the advance of a flying insect. However, on occasion, when there has been a high wind or a hurricane, the moths are spread much farther and faster. Whole forests have been attacked and the best timber trees killed by defoliation.

The gypsy moth is a medium-sized insect. The male has a wingspread of 1½ inches and the female of 2½. The male has brown wings and body and the female, which is heavier, has white wings. She lays her eggs in a buff-colored, velvety mass that is attached to trees, rocks, houses and even cars. The velvety stuff surrounding the eggs helps them to survive through the winter. In the spring they hatch and the larvae (caterpillars) then begin their work of destruction. When full grown, these larvae are 1½ to 2½ inches long, dark and hairy, with two rows of red and blue dots on their backs. In time they transform to a pupa and emerge in mid-July as adult moths, to start the cycle over again.

Gypsy moth caterpillars especially like to eat shade trees. They are very fond of oaks, especially the white oak, but will also attack evergreens and many of the other trees that ornament our towns and villages. They are attracted to birches, willows and even appletrees, and can lay waste a

Bare trees in summer, by gypsy moth

whole section of woods or forest. As they are night feeders and often lie hidden during most of the day, people sometimes are unaware of the destruction of their trees until it is too late.

The battle against the gypsy moth has been going on for almost a hundred years and in spite of all efforts, this pest continues to spread. One infestation turned up in Michigan, but was brought under control before it could do much damage. In more recent times, it has spread through Connecticut and is now in New Jersey and Pennsylvania. To a certain extent, a balance has been set up in New England. The damage to trees seems to be worse in the first attacks. Many trees, if denuded two seasons in succession, will die. But some areas seem to gain a kind of resistance, much as people do to a disease. Also, there are cycles of bad and good years, when the insect's attack on forests is more or less severe.

In the past, we have attacked the moth with chemical weapons. This culminated in the years after World War II with extensive aerial spraying of DDT. But while this deadly insecticide did achieve some good results with the gypsy moth, as with many other noxious insects, its overall effect on the environment was worse than the good it achieved. Good insects were killed along with the bad ones. The poison seeped into the soil and into our waterways and stayed there, killing fish and other forms of life. Birds were greatly affected. Many of them, like the bald eagle, became unable to lay good eggs and to raise their young, and are now threatened with extinction. So much DDT was sprayed around the world at one time that all living things, from moles to humans, now have some of this poison in their bodies. The whole world of nature has been threatened—and we still have the gypsy moth and the mosquito and other pests with us.

Fortunately, our government has banned the use of DDT and our scientists have begun work on new methods of combating the gypsy moth. One such method is the biological approach. In New Jersey, a state that has been badly damaged by the moth, a laboratory has been set up in Trenton where specialists are working on the problem. Since there are over 100 species of insects in Europe and Asia that prey on this moth, collectors have been sent abroad to bring live specimens to the lab. There they are grown and tested to see which are the most effective in battling the moth. They are also screened to be sure that they are not injurious to people (none are) or might otherwise become pests themselves. The most promising are being reared and released in areas where the moth is prevalent.

These imported parasites must also be carefully scrutinized to see if they may be carrying unwanted hitchhikers. For small as most of these flies and wasps are, they may be hosts to parasites of their own. Parasites have parasites, it seems, and it would be a sad thing if some of the new insects should bring with them enemies of the earlier imported flies and wasps that are already working on our behalf!

Different insect enemies attack the moth in different stages of its life cycle. A tiny Japanese wasp with the overpowering name of *Ooencyrtus kuwanae* searches out the moth's eggs for its attack. This wasp produces five or six generations a year, while the moth has only one.

Once the egg has become a caterpillar, there are several different insect enemies, some of which go for the younger larvae and some that specialize on the full-grown ones. Two little wasps are being used that lay their eggs inside the moth caterpillars. The wasp larvae then eat the moth larvae from within. One of the wasps lays a thousand eggs, which could presumably take care of a thousand caterpillars.

Tiny parasite lays eggs on caterpillar

There are also three species of parasitic flies that the scientists have imported for their battle against the moth. One of these dispenses with the egg stage and lays a live maggot inside the body of the caterpillar. Another species lays its egg on the body of the caterpillar. When the maggot hatches, it burrows inside. Still another unusual fly lays its egg on the leaf beside the caterpillar, which then eats it when it eats the leaf. The egg hatches into a maggot inside the caterpillar and devours its host from within.

Finally, there is a wasp that attacks the gypsy moth pupa. The egg is laid in the cocoon and the larva eats up the sleeping pupa before it can emerge as an adult moth. There are also several species of beetles that prey on the gypsy moth. Three of these are native to America and also eat other injurious insects. But one species which has been imported feeds only on gypsy moth larvae and pupae. These beetles may live four years or more and may eat well over 100 large caterpillars in a season.

Other parasitic insects are being searched for, collected and tested. Some come from India and others from Spain and Yugoslavia. In addition, bacteria are being brought into the struggle. One such, *Bacillus thuringiensis,* has been made into a "biological insecticide" known as BT. It produces a disease in the caterpillar that paralyzes its stomach so that it stops eating.

Scientists are also developing a sex attractant, synthetized from the female's sex glands, which give off a scent to attract the males. With this, the male moths are lured into traps, leaving the females unmated and infertile when the time comes to lay eggs.

In 1972 alone, the gypsy moth defoliated nearly 1.4 million acres of our forests and orchards. Now the federal government is working with the states to try to turn the tide and to keep the moth from spreading to the south. One of the most active states is New Jersey, which every season now releases millions of these new parasites to fight the moth. But success with this method will take time. Meanwhile, in specific cases, where valued decorative trees are threatened, the state will spray—but only at the request of the townspeople. More and more, the local citizens are being brought into the picture to decide what they want to have done.

Therefore, if you should go camping in the summer in woodlands that are known to be infested with the gypsy moth, look your car over carefully before you leave, and follow the suggestions of the wardens. Otherwise, you may unwittingly carry this destructive moth home with you and start a little infestation of your own. Remember, if M. Trouvelot had only been more careful, we would not now have this plague in our forests which has cost us millions and millions of dollars over the years.

Releasing parasites to fight moths

5

Lamprey's Leap

Early in the last century, it was decided to build a ship canal from Lake Ontario to Lake Erie, thus circumventing Niagara Falls and allowing shipping to pass from the St. Lawrence River and Lake Ontario into the other Great Lakes. This seemed like a good idea, and it proved very useful to the commerce that soon grew up around the Great Lakes region.

The engineers who built the canal were busy with the engineering problems involved and they failed to consider what we now call the environmental problems. They did not give a thought to the sea lamprey, a kind of fish that was native to Lake Ontario, having made its way inland up the St. Lawrence River from the Atlantic Ocean.

Most fishermen who catch a lamprey call it an eel. But it is not an eel and it is not really a fish, anymore than a whale is a fish or a bat is a bird. The lampreys and the hagfish belong to a very ancient order of sea creatures that lived 300 to 400 million years ago, even before the fishes evolved. They are the last of those pre-fishes to survive on earth.

The lamprey has a long snakelike body with two short fins

on the back. It has a slimy skin without scales and on each side of the throat is a row of seven round gill holes. It is colored a bluish gray and swims much like a snake. The most remarkable thing about it is its mouth, for it has no jaws. Instead, it has a round sucker disc, housing sharp strong teeth and a rasp of a tongue. The lamprey does not eat its prey. It fastens itself to the side of a fish with its sucker disc and sucks the blood from it. In fourteen hours it can drain the lifeblood from a fifteen-inch trout.

Although the lamprey had been living in Lake Ontario, nobody had noticed it since there had been no reports of its depredations on fish. It was not until 1890 that scientists became aware of these creatures as a threat to fish populations, and reports began to come in about fish with the round scars on their bodies, left by lamprey suckers.

The Welland Canal was opened early in the nineteenth century, but it was not until almost a hundred years later, in 1921, that the first lampreys were noted in Lake Erie. In that year, a Canadian fisherman found that he had netted an odd double catch: two fish, locked together. It was a sea lamprey attached by its sucking disc to a large lake trout. The fisherman had never seen a lamprey before, and when he took the repulsive creature to be identified, he was told that he had set a record. It was the first lamprey to be caught in Lake Erie—and the omens were not good.

Nobody took the matter as seriously as we do now. There was some argument about how the creature had got there. Had it swum through the Welland Canal on its own? Or had it attached itself to a boat and been pulled through? However it happened, everyone agreed that it had gone by way of the canal, for until then the great Niagara Falls had been an insurmountable barrier.

It was not until this monster reached Lakes Huron and Michigan that people began to realize the nature and extent of the disaster for the commercial fisheries. In Lake Erie, the lamprey did not thrive. This is because that lake is more shallow than the others. It is too warm for lampreys and the streams that run into it are not suitable as lamprey spawning grounds. We can suppose that these conditions kept the lamprey from increasing very quickly, and the damage to fish was minimal. But when these parasites found their way into Lake Huron in 1936, there occurred what fish biologists call a "lamprey explosion." They increased their numbers with amazing rapidity and fishing fell off just as precipitously.

All of the three upper Great Lakes present the best environment for the lamprey. They are deep and cold and the streams draining into them have excellent conditions for lamprey spawning. And there was a bountiful food supply. The lamprey began by attacking the big lake trout. Before 1936, the annual catch of lake trout on the American side of Lake Huron was 1,720,000 pounds. But from then onward, the catch grew smaller each year. By 1948, only 5,000 pounds of trout were taken. In a few years more, the lamprey had completely eliminated the trout from the lake!

Meanwhile, this menace spread onward throughout the lakes and began to repeat the process in Lake Michigan. In only nine years, the trout catch there fell from 5,650,000 pounds to less than 400 pounds per year. Things were so bad that by 1962, both Canada and the United States declared a closed season on lake trout. Fishing was allowed only by special permit for scientific study. And the authorities feared that the same disaster would occur in Lake Superior. With the trout gone from Lakes Huron and Michigan, biologists were counting on eventual restocking from this last of the Great Lakes. But if the supply of trout in Superior also disappeared,

Lamprey attached to fish

there would be no source left for replacements except the Great Slave Lake in northwestern Canada near the Arctic Circle.

Fishermen and fish experts were equally alarmed. A cry went up to Congress to do something before the entire fishing industry was ruined, and money was allocated for the battle against the lamprey. Soon the Fish and Wildlife Service had several research projects under way.

The first thing to be studied was the life cycle of the lamprey. Somewhere in its growth from egg to adult there must be a vulnerable point that could be attacked. The lamprey lives and grows quite differently from a fish. The eggs do not hatch into small-sized lampreys. Instead, a kind of worm emerges. This is called the larval stage. The individual remains a larva for four or five years, during which time it lives in the stream where it was spawned. Burrowing into the sand and silt, it eats microscopic creatures brought down by the current. When it has grown to be six to eight inches long, it develops eyes and a sucker disc with plenty of sharp teeth inside. Then it changes into an adult lamprey and swims downstream to the lake where it begins its life of bloodsucking on any fish it can find.

The adult phase of lamprey life lasts for a year and a half and then the spawning run begins. Males and females fight their way up the streams together in a wriggling mass. The runs take place between April and June and usually at night. Thus people are seldom aware that spawning is in progress. Once a suitable spot has been reached, the male and female lamprey work together to build a nest. They use their sucker mouths to move stones and dig a shallow hole, 3 to 6 inches deep and 12 to 30 inches wide. There the female lays her eggs which may number from 24,000 to over 100,000! Like the Pacific Coast salmon, the adult lampreys die after spawning and the eggs hatch in one to three weeks. Only one percent of the eggs will reach adulthood, but that's enough to account for the disastrous explosion of lampreys throughout the lakes.

The first efforts to control the lamprey population were made with a mechanical device. This was a weir, to be set up in the spawning streams and catch the adults on their run

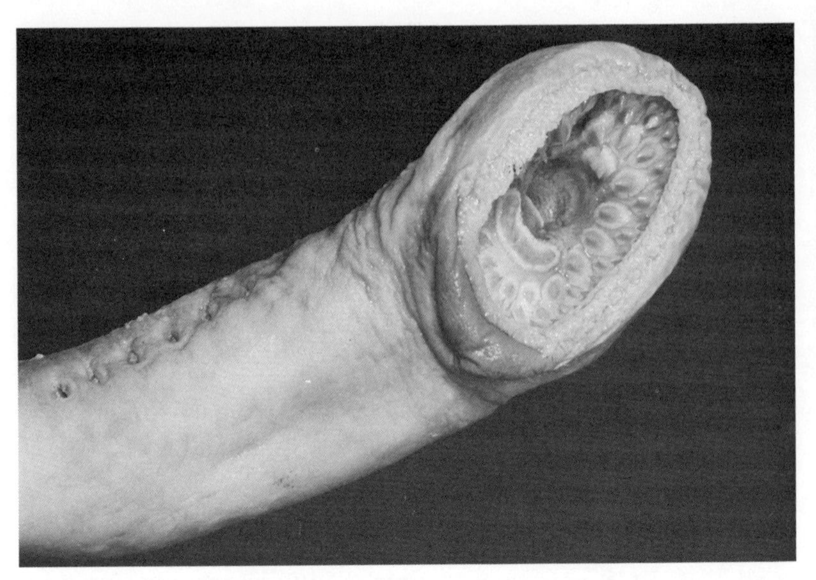

Lamprey's sucker mouth

upstream. Trout were trapped along with the lampreys and these were carefully moved upstream of the weir, where they could continue their run. The lampreys were counted, examined and killed. In one year a single weir trapped 25,000 spawning lampreys. While this was a good blow in the war against the lampreys, the outlook was dismal, considering the many, many spawning streams throughout the Great Lakes area. Superior was estimated to have 119 such streams, Michigan 108, Huron 95 and Erie 10. The prospect of operating weirs in all these streams was discouraging.

By 1951, thirty-one such traps were in operation, but they had their limitations. They were expensive to install and operate and could be damaged by ice or flood conditions. In 1952, they were beginning to be replaced by a new electrical trap. In these weirs, a row of electrodes is suspended by a cable so that they hang vertically to within a few inches of the stream bed. Lampreys and fish are repelled by the electrical field and swim into box traps on each side of the stream. If lampreys try to push through the field, they are paralyzed and collect in dead heaps below the weir. Others may swim back to the lake where they die without spawning. This system proved to be easier to operate and less expensive than the purely mechanical one.

However, even this method was not considered a perfect solution and work went on to try to discover a better one. The idea of introducing natural enemies of the lamprey, if such could be found, was vetoed. Whether it might be another vertebrate or a bacterial or viral agent, there was too much risk that it might attack the fish that the researchers were trying to save.

Instead, efforts were turned to chemical means. In the laboratory set up in northern Michigan (at Hammond Bay on Lake Huron) some 6,000 chemicals were selected for testing. The problem was to find one that would be lethal to the lamprey without harming the trout or other lake fishes. The project was set up to run fifty tests a day. In each testing jar were two lamprey, two rainbow trout and two bluegill fingerlings. They were kept in water at 55° F. and the chemical compound was added in a concentration of five parts per million. Each test was for twenty-four hours.

The first success came in 1949, when the two lamprey larvae died in a jar where the little rainbow trout and bluegills were still swimming about in good condition. By the time 4,500 such tests had been run, six chemicals had been found which gave promise of killing lampreys without harming the other fish. One compound, given the abbreviated name of TFM, was selected as being the most destructive to sea lamprey larvae. Beginning in 1958, ten spawning streams were selected around Lake Superior and treated with this chemical. Nine of these tests were very successful. In only one stream were large numbers of the larvae found after treatment. This method seemed so promising that 115 streams were treated between 1958 and 1969, 39 in Canada and 76 in the United States.

The two countries have cooperated in the war against the lamprey, pooling their resources and know-how under an international treaty known as the Great Lakes Fisheries Convention. Their efforts constitute the largest control program ever attempted against a predatory pest, and successful elimination of the lamprey will be a milestone in the history of conservation. However, complete eradication may be impossible and control methods may have to be continued to keep lamprey predation to a minimum.

With all the money being expended to control the lamprey's depredations and bring back the good lake trout to the Great Lakes, some people wonder if perhaps the lampreys could also be used for food. Centuries ago they were considered a table delicacy and King Henry VIII of England is said to have died "of a surfeit of lampreys." But whatever fascination they may have held for the gourmand king, they are no longer considered edible here and now.

The Welland Canal was built and later improved at considerable expense, but what the engineers on the project failed to take into consideration was the possible effect on the environment. Today we are learning to look into these matters before we start on a new earth-moving project. If the twentieth century costs to the fishing industry and for continued research and control of lampreys had been added to the nineteenth century expense of building the canal, the total price might have seemed more than the canal was worth.

6

The Threat of The Brazilian Bee

The Brazilian bee is a popular misnomer that has been taken over by scientists for the purpose of simplification. Originally, the honeybee (*Apis mellifera*) was native to the Old World. The New World had only some small, stingless bees, solitary bees and bumblebees, all much inferior to *A. mellifera* as a source of honey. But when Europeans came to settle in the New World, they brought the honeybee with them.

There are several different strains, or races, of honeybee, but all belong to the same species and can interbreed. The bee mostly used in America is the Italian bee (*A. m. ligustica*). There is also the German bee (*A. m. mellifera*) and the Caucasian bee (*A. m. caucasica*). All of these behave in a fairly docile manner and can be handled easily by beekeepers in the great industry that has grown up in the United States and other parts of the world.

In addition to the above, there is the African bee (*A. m. adansonii*). This bee has such a reputation for aggressiveness, making it hard to handle in an apiary, that it is seldom cultivated outside its native land. Scientists have pondered why the African bee is so quick to sting and so persistent in pursuit, and they have come up with a reasonable answer.

In Africa there is a group of birds known as the honey guides. These birds like nothing better than to feed on the contents of a bees' nest. But they are not blessed with sharp beaks and claws and so must wait until some other creature opens the nest for them. At first it was believed that the honey guide (*Indicator indicator*) was seeking the honey (as was the case with humans). But it has since been found that in reality the honey guides relish the bees' wax. They have certain bacteria in their intestines that break down the wax and help the bird to digest this strange food. Honey guides normally eat insects, but they are always on the lookout for bees, which they follow to the nest. Once they have located the hive, they set out in search of some creature that will break it open for them.

When they find a man, they light on a nearby tree branch and begin to chatter. When the man's attention is alerted, the bird flies off about fifty yards and perches again. If the man does not seem to be following, it will return and repeat the noisy signals. When it is sure that the man is following, it will fly again. Sometimes the honey seekers answer the bird with low whistles, to reassure it that they are coming. Sometimes more than one bird may be involved in the operation. When the party arrives at the bees' nest, whether in a tree or in the ground, the bird flies around in close circles, ever returning to the same spot. Soon the bees' nest is located and the angry occupants smoked out, and when the humans have gone with the honey, the bird feasts on whatever wax is left strewn about.

In addition to this predatory habit, honey guides are parasites. They lay their eggs in the nests of other birds (as do the cuckoo and the cowbird), and the baby birds have special hooks on their beaks with which they tear up the original nestlings and throw them out of the nest. But in spite, or because of, these unpleasant habits, the honey guide is highly regarded in Africa. It is said that in earlier times the native chiefs would cut off the ear of any man who killed a honey guide.

Honey Badgers

Man is not the only creature that follows the honey guide to the bees' nest. There is also a small animal, called the honey badger (*Mellivora capensis*) with strong claws and a tough hide, that also appreciates honey. If there are no people available, the honey guide will lead this badger to the tree, and it has been theorized that it was probably doing so long before man evolved on the African continent. In fact, this behavior must have been going on for millions of years and very likely is responsible for the quick temper and aggressiveness of the African bee, which is quick to attack anything that threatens its nest.

So it is not surprising that African bees were not one of the strains originally brought to this country. However, in 1956 some Brazilian scientists, believing that a tropical bee might do a better job in their country, imported 47 queen bees of *A. m. adansonii.* The idea was to cross them with the European bees then in the country and thus to build a better bee for the Brazilian apiarists.

The scientists were aware of the undesirable traits of the African bees and the experimental hives were equipped with special guards whereby the worker bees could go in and out but the queens and the drones could not. Since worker bees cannot form a new hive and propagate themselves, this would prevent the escape of the bees into the wild. However, in 1957 a visiting beekeeper, who did not understand about these guards (called double queen excluders) made the mistake of removing them, and twenty-six African queens, followed by their swarms, escaped into the countryside!

The scientists who have been studying the problem do not believe that the queens were of the pure African strain, since all but one of them came from South Africa, where African bees have long been mixed with European imports. Nevertheless, there seemed to be enough of the African genes in these bees to start causing problems within a short period. Since the escaped bees were not pure African bees, they have become known as Brazilian bees.

It did not take the immigrant bees long to spread out across the huge territory that is Brazil. Since they are tropical bees, they were inclined to move north into the tropical jungles. To

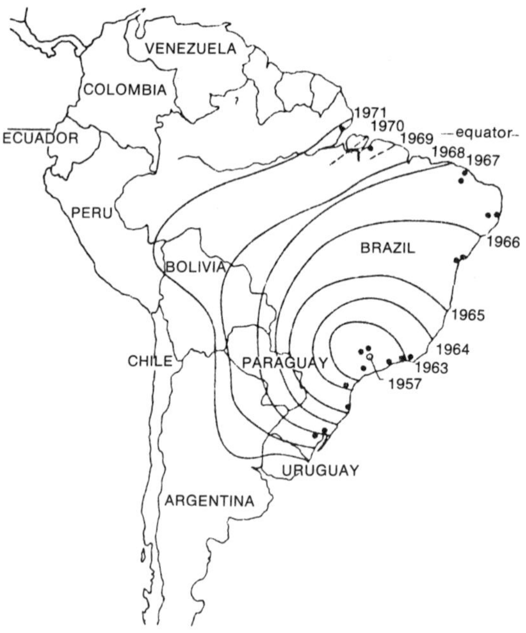

The steady spread of the imported African honeybee through South America is shown in this map taken from a report to the Department of Agriculture by the National Academy of Sciences/ National Research Council. (Kerr/NAS/NRC)

Spread of Brazilian bees, 1957–1971

the south they have invaded Uruguay, Paraguay, Bolivia and northern Argentina. But they seem to be stopped by the colder regions, unable to overwinter successfully. Still, their march northward seems to be progressing at a steady rate. By 1970, they had crossed the equator, and there seems to be nothing to keep them from marching up the Isthmus of Panama into Central America and the United States. When we note the comparable lands occupied south of the equator, it appears that they would be right at home in Florida, New Orleans and probably as far north as Los Angeles.

What is this going to do to the very active bee industry in our southern states? And what is it going to do to the people who live in those states? The Brazilian bee has been reported to take over the hives and the territory of the old European bees as it invades new areas. It enters the hives of the European bees, and soon the beekeeper finds that he has a swarm of aggressive Brazilian bees instead of his previously docile European bees.

Brazilian bees are much harder to manage than the European bee under the usual management practices. They get upset by the slightest disturbance to their hives, and it takes a lot more smoke to quiet them and a lot more time and patience to perform the required work at the hive. They are not only extremely sensitive to disturbances, but they communicate their alarm more quickly within the hive and to adjacent hives, and they quickly bring a massive attack against any intruder. It is believed that they are more sensitive than other bees to the alarm pheromones (chemical scent signals) released by bees. Or possibly they release more such pheromones than do European bees.

In spite of these drawbacks, many Brazilian beekeepers were found to prefer the new Brazilian bees. They say they are far more productive than the European bees, making from 1.25 to 2 times as much honey as the Italian bees under similar circumstances. One reason for this is that Brazilian bees seem to work harder. They get out in the fields up to two hours earlier in the morning and work as much later in the evenings, often until full darkness. They also waste no time in hovering about the hive entrance, but rush right in. Moreover, they

Brazilian bees on comb

have been proved to carry heavier loads, in spite of the fact that they are smaller than the Italian bees.

These characteristics may offset their aggressive behavior in the minds of some Brazilian apiarists. But others say that in the cooler weather zones to the south the bees consume so much more honey just to keep going that it negates their great productivity. And some scientists believe that productivity depends as much on the size of the honey flow in the fields and the amount of competition from other bees (wild bees included) as upon the individual efforts of the bees.

There is no difference between the sting of the Brazilian bee and that of other bees, but they sting more quickly and in greater numbers and they follow the "intruder" a greater distance from the hive. While a swarm of Italian bees may sting at the rate of 10 times a minute, (that is, 10 bees a minute), an African hive might deliver 200 to 300 stings a minute. Reports from Brazil cite a rise in deaths from bee stings and a rise in the number of animals being stung. Recent records mention from 200 to 300 deaths from bee stings in Brazil as compared with 100 in the United States. All this bodes ill for the American bee industry. The average person is afraid of bees as it is, and beekeeping has been banned from many city environments. Beekeepers are often sued if people or animals get badly stung. The Brazilian bee could put many apiarists out of business, or at least change some practices of the industry.

There are several different facets of the American bee industry. Honey and wax are not the only benefits that the bee bestows on humanity. Far more important is the job they do in pollinating important crops. Without bees, we would lose many of our favorite foods. Even flowering plants would suffer. In this century a whole big industry has developed based on the bee's importance as a pollinator. Beekeepers move their hives about with the seasons. Just as migratory workers move about to harvest the crops, beekeepers bring their hives to the fields and orchards in the early spring when the crops need to be pollinated. To do this, the hives are closed and loaded upon trucks or into airplanes and moved long distances. But how will the Brazilian bee take to this kind of hive disturbance? Queens would have to be moved in separate cages, because when the Brazilian bees are disturbed to this extent, they sometimes form a ball around the queen and kill her!

Another facet of the bee industry is shipping packaged queens to customers around the country. Bees cannot winter well in our northern states and in Canada, so apiarists there buy new queens, often sent with a small group of workers, each spring. When they find they are getting aggressive Brazilian bees instead of docile European bees, they will probably stop buying from producers in our southern states and will order from Europe instead.

Most apiarists set out their hives on little stands, all in a row. But Brazilian beekeepers now find that they must put a fair distance between hives. The new bees have a great tendency to abscond. At the least disturbance or for some unknown reason, they will take off with their queen and depart for the wilds. If the hives are situated close together, not only does a disturbance arouse aggressive behavior in all the hives, but if one hive absconds, the others nearby may follow.

It is easy to see that the arrival of Brazilian bees in this country is likely to cost the bee industry a lot of money, if nothing worse. Greater space will be needed in order to spread out the hives. More time must be taken in handling the bees, and time is money in industry. More lawsuits are likely to result from bee stings, and more restrictive laws will be passed by governing bodies. And what will happen to the pollinating part of the industry is anybody's guess.

With the steady advance northward of the new Brazilian bees looking like a tornado cloud on our southern horizon, apiarists and bee scientists are working to find some solution before the bees actually arrive. A committee of eminent scientists, appointed by the National Research Council, went to South America to study the situation. Their report was published in 1972. In almost every aspect of the problem, they call for more research. While many new things have been learned about bees in this century, most of the work has been done on such aspects as bee communication. The fascinating dances of the bees have been described by such famous scientists as Karl Von Frisch. But little work has been done

Scientists studying Brazilian bees

on aggressiveness and genetics. Now such research is urgently needed.

The first action to be put into effect, the committee says, is a rigid quarantine against African bees. One queen let loose in the country could negate all other work. All North and Central American countries must establish rigid rules against the importation of any African bee material, in any life stage, including semen. This quarantine must be enforced against all countries to which African bees may have been introduced.

We must also learn how to identify the Brazilian bee quickly and inexpensively in the field, in preparation for the time when it may begin to infiltrate the country. It is slightly smaller than the European bee, but this is not a very exact identification. It has been suggested that bee dances vary among the different strains of *Apis mellifera* much as languages differ among humans, and that perhaps an exact identification can be developed along such lines.

It is hoped that some kind of barrier—physical or chemical—may be devised to prevent the bees from passing into Central or North America. This will take a lot of research. Insecticides are an obvious chemical barrier, but the unfortunate pollution effects resulting from indiscriminate use of such poisons are well known. Nobody wants to repeat that mistake. Another suggestion is the trapping and destruction of wild swarms, but the accomplishment of such an undertaking throughout the jungles to the south of us would seem to be a difficult one.

Another possibility is the genetic angle. It has been suggested that the release of millions of drone bees, bred especially for nonaggressive, nonswarming, nonabsconding tendencies, in the barrier area might supplant the regular Brazilian drones in the mating flights to fertilize the queens. This might perhaps breed out the undesirable traits from the invading bees. But there is always the chance that the Brazilian drones may prove to be more aggressive than the European drones in the mating flights, in which case this approach would be impractical.

The Brazilian bee may not reach our shores from South America for another ten to twenty years, but when it does, we had better be ready for it. Otherwise, when you go for a picnic in any of our southern states, or just take an afternoon's ramble through the woods, and happen to fall over a wild bees' nest, the results may be much worse than you expect. The cloud of angry bees pursuing you would inflict more stings and follow you much farther than would be the case today. And if you have an allergy to bee sting, you might not leave the spot alive.

IV

WITH WILLFULL INTENT

7

The Weed That Never Stops Growing

The water hyacinth (*Eichhornia crassipes*) is as good an example of evil disguised as elegance as you will find in the whole plant kingdom. In its native haunts in South America, not much was said against it. Explorers looking for exotic plants noticed the beautiful, delicate blooms of this water plant and collected some to take home to the United States. We have been paying for that mistake ever since.

In 1884, the plant was shown here at a horticultural exhibition. The lavender and pale lilac spikes of the flowerlets were a big hit, and people began to plant water hyacinths in their garden pools. Soon it proved to be impossible to confine it to such spots. It was introduced into Florida in 1890 and by 1897 it was choking up the state's waterways.

The story of the water hyacinth reads like a science fiction tale of some menace from outer space arriving to take over the world. But in this case, it came only from as far away as South America and we brought it here ourselves! One thing leading to its quick spread throughout our southern states is its rapid rate of reproduction. In one experiment, it was found that two parent hyacinths could produce 30 young plants in twenty-three days, and at the end of four months, they had increased that amount to 1,200! Plants can flower at the end of twenty-six days and will then produce seeds—anywhere up to 5,000 seeds per plant. Seeds fall to the bottom of the lake or river and can still sprout after fifteen years. From this it is easy to see how one plant could become a serious problem to a river or canal in a short time.

Elegant flowers of water hyacinths

Water hyacinths travel by various means. They are free-floating plants and the upright leaves act as sails so that they can be blown hither and yon across the water, setting up new colonies wherever they come to rest. Seeds lying in the mud of streams may become attached to the legs of birds or animals and thus moved from place to place. It is also believed that water birds may carry the seeds long distances, even thousands of miles in the case of migratory birds. Sometimes the plants become tangled around the propellers of ships and are carried many miles. When the ship reaches port, the engines are reversed in docking and the plant falls off, quite able to start a new infestation in the new waters.

In the United States, these huge rafts of plants make trouble for ships and smaller boats; for the lumber industry, when timber is floated down rivers; and for fishermen. As the water hyacinth grows, its lower leaves die and fall off. These sink to the bottom, building a layer of debris which clogs the waterway below, while the living plants are clogging the water above. Rivers have been closed to boats when control measures were not regularly carried out. Marinas and fishing camps have had to close, often permanently, when their customers could not get to them.

You might think that the rest of the world would profit by our unfortunate experience and refuse to admit the water hyacinth into their lands. But such has not been the case. Time after time, people succumbed to the lure of the beautiful blossoms, and now the water hyacinth is running rampant in all the tropical lands around the globe. It is causing trouble in Africa and Asia, in Australia and New Zealand.

In the rivers of Africa, it was especially troublesome, because the people of Africa use the rivers for travel and communication. And yet the people who are most affected have been remarkably careless about spreading the plant. Boats of all kinds drag the plants up and down the rivers, causing new infestations. Natives often pick the plants to use as cushions in their canoes and then throw them out when no longer needed. Then too, the rivers help to spread the plants, flushing them out of backwaters and swamps at flood time, when whole islands of the weed will be swept downstream.

Water hyacinths spread 1,000 miles along the Congo River between 1952 and 1954.

On the Nile River, the plant has been equally destructive. The problem has been chiefly in the White Nile. Due to efficient quarantine, it has been kept out of the Blue Nile, which joins the White Nile at Khartoum. But Egypt spends $1.5 million yearly in an effort to keep the Nile clear.

In addition to halting navigation, the weed also makes trouble for the new hydroelectric plants and dams that have been built along the rivers in recent years. Not only do leaves and roots clog up the machinery and irrigation ditches, but the plant itself uses large amounts of water, and the large leaves evaporate water at a much faster rate than would the surface of the water itself. Thus, the water needed for irrigation and electric power is used and wasted by this plant parasite upon the river.

Since the end of the last century, millions of dollars have been spent yearly just to keep the water hyacinth down to nuisance levels. Eradication is apparently impossible. The first methods were mechanical with the use of dredges. Throughout our southern states, the waterways were kept clear by constant dredging and digging. But it often seemed that by the time one end of the river was clean, the other end would be clogged up again. William E. Wunderlich, aquatic growth control chief of the New Orleans District of the Army's Corps of Engineers, says that you can never let up. "I've seen a 300-horsepower tug stopped tight by water hyacinth," he declared. "I've seen grown men walking on it!"

More recently, a chemical weed killer, known as 2,4-D, has been used to fight the water hyacinth. It has proved very successful and is being used in other countries. However, it has drawbacks. It is harmful to other vegetation, and so must be used with care. As we have learned from the DDT experience, it is dangerous to release large amounts of a lethal chemical into the environment without knowing what the effect will be on the whole ecology.

Another form of control that has been tried in our southern states is the manatee. Manatees, or sea cows, are large, water-living, herbivorous mammals. They are becoming rather rare. In fact, one species, Steller's sea cow, has been entirely killed off. It was hunted to extinction between the years 1741 and 1768. Our native species in Florida is disappearing too, partly from wanton killing and partly from loss of habitat. Now it has been found that the sea cow loves to eat water hyacinth. An adult can consume between 60 and 100 pounds of weed in a day. Placed in a southern canal, it will soon clear out the water plants. But unfortunately, there are not many sea cows left. And unlike the water hyacinth, they do not reproduce quickly. Two manatees, in an experiment, were placed together in a tank, and after two years, they still had not mated and produced young.

However, it seems likely that a tank may not be the best environment for manatee courtship. For thousands of years, wild cheetahs have been tamed by the potentates of Asia and Africa, yet they never became domestic animals because they would not breed in captivity. But in recent years, scientists studying the behavior of these cats have realized that they are essentially solitary beasts. In zoos (and in ancient palaces, no doubt) they were kept together in one enclosure, in violation of their natural instincts. Then an Italian zoo tried the experiment of introducing a strange cheetah to a female in season, with the happy result of a litter of cubs. Now cheetahs are being bred in zoos around the world and the animal is no longer in danger of extinction. Perhaps when some dedicated scientist makes an in-depth study of the manatee, he will discover what conditions are needed to trigger the breeding instinct, and we will then begin to have sufficient sea cows to help with the control of the water hyacinth.

Still another drawback to relying on the manatee to clear the waterways for us is the resurgence of the alligator. For a number of years now the alligator has been on the endangered species list because of wanton killing by hunters and poachers, who sold their hides to the leather industry. But now that the animal has been protected by a national ban on such activities, it has begun to increase in numbers once again and has become a threat to manatees introduced into the Florida waterways to clear out the weeds. Not long ago, a ranger watched a mother sea cow with twin calves, feeding in a canal. He was startled to see an alligator rise to the surface and grab one of the babies. With all these problems, it seems doubtful that the manatee can increase its numbers sufficiently to be of much help in eradicating the water hyacinth.

Another control method now being studied is the use of weed-eating fishes. One of these is the Chinese grass carp (*Ctenopharyngodon idella*). It lives in the lakes and rivers of Siberia and Manchuria and is cultivated by the Russians as a food fish. Others are two species of cichlids, a perchlike fish with the scientific name of *Tilapia*. One of these comes from Java and the other from the Congo. All these fish are being carefully studied to see which might do the best job of weed control and which might adapt best to our southern waters, and to be sure that none of them might become a pest or a threat to our native fishes. Unfortunately, it seems that with all three fish species, the water hyacinth is far down on their list of preferred waterweed diet. So control by fish is still in the experimental stage.

Altogether, the problem of keeping our waterways free of

Hyacinths clog drainage ditches

this invader is an expensive one. In 1956, the southern states of Florida, Alabama, Mississippi and Louisiana spent $43 million on the project. Perhaps this is why in the South it is called the "million-dollar weed." Yet in spite of this history and the fact that we have laws against transporting it across state lines, it still appears in catalogs selling water garden plants.

There is even an organization of the people who work at the job of controlling this parasite, the Hyacinth Control Society. At a meeting in 1965, the members agreed that in addition to everything else, the plant is unpredictable. Sometimes it grows below a dam and not above it, although usually it likes to fill up the waters that the dam impounds. Sometimes, when it has been eradicated, it will not come back, but all too often this is not the case.

One botanist, Dr. E. C. S. Little, of Britain, in spite of all this, can find some good in the plant. He says that it might be a new source of food and that it has the same nutritional value as the turnip. With the world food situation in crisis, this may be good news. A plant so prolific and indestructible, that grows almost anywhere—it has recently developed an ability to grow in salt water!—may just possibly in the future turn out to be a help rather than a hindrance.

8

Too Much of a Good Thing

The pigeon was brought to America for good, practical reasons, as a domestic bird and for use as a messenger. But many wild birds were imported only for sentimental reasons. Chances are, if such an exotic importation manages to survive the rigors of the new environment, it will in time become a pest. This is the history of two European species, the house sparrow and the starling, brought to this country in the last century and universally regretted ever since.

The house sparrow (*Passer domesticus*), usually called the English sparrow, originated in Africa. Its relatives still living there are called weaver birds and they build remarkable nests, like round, woven baskets. Sometimes one tree will have a group of these nests hanging from different branches, where the birds enter through little holes in the bottom or side. During its long travels, the house sparrow seems to have lost some of this nest-building technique and the nests it builds from twigs are much less spectacular.

The ancestors of the house sparrow wandered away from their original haunts in the interior of Africa and eventually reached the Nile Valley at some time during the Pleistocene Age (one million to twenty thousand years ago). This period in the earth's history was marked by succeeding ice ages, and the sparrows that got as far as the Iberian peninsula or Italy were cut off there during the ice ages. Occasionally there were interglacial periods, when the ice would melt, and then the various groups of sparrows would get together again and interbreed. Little by little, these sparrows spread around the Mediterranean.

By the end of the last ice age, when the sparrows were once again able to spread out into new areas, a different situation had developed. Man had begun to settle down, to build farms and villages and to raise grain. The seed-eating sparrows found this very much to their liking. They moved right in with the farmers, made nests close to the houses, and fed on the bits of grain left in the fields or dropped around the farm.

With the ice melting everywhere to the north, people began to move into northern Europe. They took the new food-raising techniques with them, and the sparrows followed right along. So from earliest times, this little bird has been associated with people. It has found a living both in the country and

House sparrow

the city and is well accustomed to humans. Today it is considered a commensal of man—a table companion, since it shares our food. It's an unusual house sparrow that nests very far from human habitation.

Sparrows were originally country birds, following the farmer as he sowed his seed or reaped the grain. But in later years it moved into the cities, where it found its food in the grain dropped from the horses' feed bags and in garbage left around the streets. British farmers heartily disliked the sparrow, claiming that it ate a high percentage of their grain. They thought Americans must be crazy to want to import it, and as it turned out, they were right. But there was a sentimental attachment to the sparrow, which seemed so much a part of the English countryside that Americans had left behind, and in 1850 efforts were begun to introduce the sparrow to this country.

At the Brooklyn Institute, a committee was set up to arrange for the importation of sparrows. They were cared for in a large cage during the winter and released in the spring of 1851. But they did not survive, and the Brooklyn bird lovers, ignoring this gesture of fate, collected $200 and sent Nicholas Pike to England to get some more. In 1852, he dispatched a larger group of sparrows to the Institute. They were released in Greenwood Cemetery in the spring of 1853. The Institute even hired a man to watch over them! This time the effort was successful. The birds began to breed and increase their numbers.

The Brooklyn group was not the only one interested in bringing Europe's songbirds to America. (The sparrow was one of the few such imports that survived and made an impact on the new land.) Sparrows were being introduced in Maine and Rhode Island. In the 1860s, sparrows were released on Boston Common and in New York's Central Park. They were even sent as far afield as San Francisco, Salt Lake City and Quebec. Sparrows are known to be insect eaters, as well as grain feeders, and they were brought to some towns especially to counteract a plague of caterpillars. But the caterpillars were different from the ones the sparrows were used to in England. They were covered with hairs which stuck in the birds' throats. Instead of controlling the caterpillars, the sparrows drove away the native robins, orioles and cuckoos, which would normally have done the job.

By the 1880s, America's attitude toward the sparrow had changed drastically. People began to realize that they had a pest instead of an ornament. Laws which had protected the sparrow were repealed and bounties were instituted. Sparrow

Sparrow bathing

clubs were formed and "sparrow money" collected to pay people to kill the birds and destroy the nests containing eggs or nestlings. In some cities, sparrows were sold on the market and put into meat pies.

But the sparrow is a remarkably hardy bird and quickly restored its numbers to fill in these losses. Since the automobile has supplanted the horse, the birds are not seen in such numbers in the cities. This is not only because they can no longer snatch the horses feed, but because while hopping in the streets they soil their feet with motor oil. The oil then smears the sparrows' eggs as they sit on the nest. It clogs the shell pores and the baby birds cannot hatch!

Sparrows are still quite active in rural and suburban areas. Besides eating the farmer's corn, they have been accused of destroying decorative plants and the buds of fruit trees in the spring. By nesting in trees and vines, they kill these plants with their excrement. They are noisy birds, and the chattering of their flocks annoys householders. And although they are said to take a great many insects during their nesting period when the baby birds are fed an insect diet, this hardly makes up for the damage they do in other ways. Finally, they are accused of driving away the beneficial native birds and taking over their nests. Every bird lover who maintains a feeding tray will attest to the fact that when the sparrows arrive, the other birds vanish.

In spite of being such a little bird, the sparrow has a high IQ. Its brain is proportionately large for its size, and it is quick to take advantage of any opportunity offered it in a new environment. Most birds act from instinct, but the sparrow occasionally does things that seem to show intelligence of a sort. They have been seen to follow various predators, such as cats, keeping just out of reach and proclaiming the danger to the rest of the flock. And while most small birds will not notice when their nests are parasitized by a cowbird, the sparrow seems to be aware that the new egg is not its own. Experiments made at the Patuxent Wildlife Research Center in Maryland in 1964 confirmed this. Five sparrow eggs were removed from a nest and five phoebe eggs substituted. The mother sparrow incubated the new eggs for two days but then abandoned the nest.

Sparrows stay in their area all winter. And while their numbers have decreased somewhat since 1913, due partly to the arrival of the automobile and partly to competition with the starling, these little birds are still with us and likely to remain so. They have extended their range throughout the United States and Canada and into Mexico and South America. Scientists think it is only a matter of time before they will have spread to Siberia, China, and throughout Australia.

> Nay,
> I'll have a starling shall be taught to speak
> Nothing but Mortimer.

If Shakespeare had not put these words into his play *Henry IV,* we might not now be spending thousands of dollars yearly to get rid of starlings. For although many people tried to import the bird from Europe, none of their efforts were successful until Eugene Scheifflin took a hand in the project in 1890.

Scheifflin was a drug manufacturer who had made lots of money in his business and so could afford to indulge in hobbies. And his two major interests were birds and Shakespeare. Apparently, believing that the New World was deficient in bird life, he decided to bring to America every bird that is mentioned by the Bard. Most of these attempts were failures. Birds like the skylark and the nightingale could not adjust to the new environment. But the starling was a different matter.

The starling *(Sturnus vulgaris)* was much admired in Europe for centuries. Its natural range was from England to Siberia for breeding in the summer, and south to the Mediterranean for the winter. An individual starling is a handsome bird with glossy black feathers, a short, square tail and bright yellow beak. It struts around in an aggressive manner and does not hop as do many birds. Being related to the mynah bird of India, it has that bird's ability to mimic any sound and thus can be taught to talk in the same way as parrots and parakeets. For this reason it was often a prized pet, and

Starling carrying beetle to nest

Samuel Pepys, writing in his diary in 1668, mentions "a starling which do whistle and talk the most and best that ever I heard."

So why is the starling now considered a pest? Simply because there are too many of them. They are more intelligent than many birds and are able to adapt to a variety of living conditions. They can change their eating habits to take advantage of whatever food source is available. And as they have spread around the world (with the assistance of man) they have increased their numbers phenomenally.

One objection to the starling is that the birds gather in huge flocks to roost, where they are both dirty and noisy. There are also complaints about them on the agricultural front, where they have developed into a pest of major proportions, being accused of eating corn and fruit. In more recent years, they have become a hazard at airports, as they may roost in the shrubbery near the runways. The swooping flocks have been caught in the propellers or sucked into the motors of jets.

The year was 1890 when Scheifflin released his birds in Central Park, New York City, and they immediately began nesting. The first starling nest in the New World was reported from the American Museum of Natural History, where it had been constructed under the eaves of the building.

At first the spread of starlings was slow. The flocks in New York City increased and people began to complain about the droppings, but it was not until the early part of this century that they were noticed outside of New York. In 1916 they turned up in Ohio. By 1920 they were in Kentucky and Illinois. They were in Utah by 1935, and Colorado by 1938. By the middle of the century they had covered much of the country and ventured into southern Canada. It was estimated that there were 50 million starlings on the North American continent. Today they have reached Alaska and are found in all of the fifty states. They are believed to be the most numerous birds in the country.

The starling seems to vary its behavior according to the season. It likes to spend the winter in the city, where it can roost in sheltered spots among the tall buildings, often taking advantage of the heat from chimneys or airducts. They fly out every day to the suburbs and the country, where they find food (though they are not above eating garbage in the city itself) and return at sunset to their roosting sites. The area below these roosts soon builds up with dirty droppings, and the noise of the returning flocks at evening is an irritation to the citizens.

In the summer, these roosts are apt to be deserted as the birds move to the suburbs or country to find nesting holes and to raise their babies—often two broods a season. It is then that they run afoul of the farmers and gardeners, whose crops they pillage.

Communities that are favored with a starling roost usually lose no time in urging the authorities to do something about it, and a variety of starling discouragements have been tried out. None has proven to be perfect, and the end result seems to be that the birds are merely frightened into moving their roost a few miles away, where somebody else will suffer from them.

In some cities, returning starlings have been blasted with shotguns (a doubtful method, as people are apt to get shot, too). Electrical wires have been installed on window ledges. Roosts have been treated with itching powder, grease, bubble spray. Fake owls, stink bombs and roman candles have been used to scare the birds. Perhaps the most successful method has been the bio-acoustical technique, developed in this country and now used around the world. In this method, a captured starling is held—usually by a leg or a wing—in front of a recording device, and its cries of alarm are thus recorded and put on tape. The tape is then played back over a loud speaker at the roosting site. This usually has the desired effect of scaring the entire flock away. The method is now used at airports, but officials also recommend the elimination of all trees, shrubs and other growth near the runways where the birds might roost. Certainly, cutting down the trees in a pleasant country town is a drastic and undesirable last resort, but in some cases it has been the only thing that has worked.

When considered impartially, the starling is really a model in successful bird behavior. It has many traits that we admire in ourselves. They are devoted parents and the male does his share of the work. He even builds the nest, to which he later brings the female he has courted. He takes turns in sitting on the eggs and feeding the nestlings.

As long as the starling was a country bird, it was very clean, taking frequent baths in pools or streams. But when it became a city bird, such ablutions went by the board. And when the huge flocks took to roosting on city buildings, depositing great quantities of droppings, the starling acquired a reputation as a very dirty bird.

Originally an insect eater, the starling was welcomed by farmers and gardeners. They are credited with destroying great quantities of Japanese and potato beetles. One hundred years ago, English naturalists insisted that starlings ate only insects. They don't like grain or fruit, said the officials. And as late as 1921, a scientific report stated that the starling, among all the birds of northeastern America, was one of the best destroyers of terrestrial insects.

But transplanted to this country, where their numbers built up into huge flocks, the starlings took to eating anything they could find. Grain and fruit went on their menu in a hurry. They were seen to feast on potatoes, roots, snails and even lizards. In the cities, they took to eating garbage. A flock of hungry starlings has been known to strip a tree of leaves.

Like the sparrow, the starling is a bird with a high IQ. The proportion of brain to overall size is much larger than in most

Starling

birds. This probably accounts for its remarkable adaptation to any habitat or food supply. Also for its uncommon ability to mimic other birds and sounds. Naturalists have found that they can determine which species of birds live in a certain area simply by listening to a starling. And they do not confine themselves to imitating the sounds of other birds. The starling is believed to have spread so quickly across the country simply by imitating the migration habits of other birds.

These highly social birds seem to use more than just alarm cries to communicate. Students of poisonous insects, such as the monarch butterfly, have observed that a starling that has tasted such fare and found it unpalatable will go through a ritual of wiping its beak. It will do this when presented with the obnoxious insect a second time, and another bird, watching, will also wipe its beak and refuse the insect.

Today the government maintains two research centers for the study of starlings and other "problem" birds: at Patuxent, Maryland, and at Denver, Colorado. Scientists there are still looking for the answer to the burgeoning starling population and for a satisfactory method of controlling it.

In the experiment of introducing foreign eggs into a bird's nest, starlings were used as well as sparrows, and the results were similar. The starlings threw the strange eggs out of their nests and refused to rear the young. So the starling, like the sparrow, seems to be immune to parasitism by such birds as the cuckoo in Europe and the cowbird in America. All in all, the starling is a smart bird. Now that we have brought him to the New World, there is still the question whether he may outsmart us in the end.

9

The Prickly Peril

The cactus is another plant that has made the grand tour around the world with our assistance—and at our expense. Cacti were originally only American plants. Only one species is credited with being a native of North Africa, and that one probably got there from South America, carried by a bird.

The evolution of the cactus can be traced by study of the plants now living in the Americas, back to their beginnings 50 million years ago. At that time the world's climate was generally warm and tropical, and the ancestors of the cactus resembled citrus trees. Plants of this kind can still be found growing in the West Indies. When in the course of the millennia, great mountain chains were thrust up along the continents, these cut off the rainfall and desert areas appeared. The change was gradual, and the cactus species living in those areas gradually adapted. Those that could not adapt died out, but the ones that survived developed in different ways into strange and marvelous plants.

Cacti are found the whole length of the Americas, from the Arctic Circle to the tip of Patagonia. During the process of evolution, they lost their leaves and developed thick, woody stems or trunks in which they could store water during the increasing dry periods. Some became mere round balls and others developed grotesque forms. To protect themselves from plant-eating animals looking for a bit of green in the growing desert, the cacti developed spikes and spines.

There seems to be no limit to the versatility of the cacti. They are able to survive in the high mountains at altitudes where the air is thin. In the far north they endure temperatures of −40° and −50°F., and in the desert sun they can withstand heat as great as 140°F. They have even gone back to the warm, moist jungles, the seeds probably carried by birds. There they have become tree-living species, or epiphytes (air plants), living like orchids on the branches of trees and getting their nourishment from the moisture in the atmosphere.

There are five traits that distinguish a cactus. First, they all possess a special structure on their stems and branches called an areole which has two buds. The lower bud grows spines and the upper one new branches or flowers. Second, cacti are perennial; they do not die at the end of one season. Third, their flowers are wheel-shaped or funnel-shaped and the fruit always grows below the flower. Fourth, the fruit is a one-celled berry with the seeds scattered through it. And fifth, cactus seeds always produce two embryo leaves when they germinate. A cactus must have all these qualities. If a plant lacks even one, it is not a cactus.

Cacti can grow as tall as trees, like the giant saguaro and the organ pipe cactus of our southwest. They can be small round plants, bristling with prickers, like the pincushion cactus or the star cactus. In some, the prickles have evolved into long silky hairs. There are over 2,000 species of cacti and all were bizarre and unearthly in form to European eyes. No wonder that they have been given such names as Old Man Cactus, Grizzly Bear, Bunny Ears and Prickly Pear.

The first explorers to set eyes on cacti could hardly believe what they saw. These plants looked like no known vegetation of the Old World. They seemed to belong to another world—as indeed they did, since the New World was completely unknown to Europeans until the voyages of Columbus.

Soon the explorers began to send cactus plants back to

Europe as curiosities of America and a fad developed for cultivating these odd plants. Presently it was discovered that the plants had their uses. The Indians, it turned out, had learned many ways in which the plants could benefit them. They were used by the Indians to produce food, drugs, drink and timber.

Cactus garden

The cactus most favored by the Europeans at first was the prickly pear, a member of the Opuntia family. The fruit of this cactus can be eaten and soon it was being cultivated in Spain, Portugal and the countries of the Mediterranean. From there it spread to India and southern Asia, where it became an important food crop. Opuntias had several uses. They not only provided food for people, but were also the food plant for the valued cochineal insect, used in making red dyes. Whole industries were built up around this insect, and so the opuntias became very important. In addition, their striking forms and beautiful flowers made them popular decorative plants.

By the nineteenth century, Opuntias were being grown for these reasons in South Africa, Madagascar, India, Ceylon and Australia, and in all these places they showed a tendency to spread wildly and become pests. This was especially true of Australia in the provinces of Queensland and New South Wales. Some twenty species of Opuntia had been transplanted to foreign countries and nine of these had a tendency to become pests. The two most dangerous were *O. inermis* and *O. stricta.* In the 1880s, they were beginning to alarm the authorities and by 1900 they had taken over 10 million acres in Australia.

Opuntias spread by various means. Shoots, broken off from the main plant, could be blown along till they found a new spot to gain a foothold. Seeds also dispersed easily. The fruit proved agreeable to the Australian birds and animals, and thus the seeds were spread far and wide. The seeds were hard-shelled, not easily destroyed, and sprouted quickly after heavy rain. In fact, Opuntia seeds can germinate after lying dormant for twenty years!

More and more farm and pasture land was being taken over by these foreign plants, and the Australian farmers fought back with every means they could think of. The Opuntias were crushed with rollers, torn up with machines, poisoned with chemicals and burned with fire. But to no avail. The plants continued to take over more land. Commissions were set up to study the problem. Scientists came to North and South America, looking for disease and insect enemies of the Opuntias. Oddly enough, one such enemy, a scale insect, was

Rabbit Ears cacti

found in Ceylon, not the original home of the cacti. This cactus parasite was brought to Australia, bred in large quantities and strewn about the fields. It did wipe out one species of Opuntia, *O. monacantha,* in a few years. But unfortunately, it had no effect at all upon the two most damaging species. In 1925, *O. inermis* took over 40 million acres in Queensland and 7 million acres in New South Wales, and *O. stricta* devastated 10 million acres!

But the scientists kept on looking, and in the Americas they found 150 different insects that attack cacti on their home ground. Fifty of these were selected and sent to Australia, where they were carefully tested. It was especially important that they should not release an insect that might itself become a pest, while trying to find something to fight the plant pest. And finally, the right insect was found. A moth *(Cactoblastis cactorum)* was brought from Argentina. The caterpillar of this moth lives in the shoots of Opuntias and destroys them. This moth proved to be an effective control on the two worst Opuntia pests, and during the 1930s their colonies began to shrink. More and more land was reclaimed. And the people who had brought this disaster upon themselves owed their deliverance to a little moth!

Just as in the case of the water hyacinth, complete extermination proved to be impossible. People in Australia continue to grow Opuntias as decorative plants and the birds continue to eat the fruits and to carry the seeds far and wide. New colonies of this menace start up here and there. And whenever there is a particularly heavy rainfall, the old seeds, lying unnoticed, germinate and start this transplanted monster on its path of conquest again.

In South Africa, another Opuntia, *O. megacantha,* became a difficult pest. This species grows as large as a tree, as do many of the pest Opuntias. It was introduced as long ago as 1750, having been brought by the Dutch East India Company from India. People ate its fruit and also planted it as a hedge around the *kraals* (cattle enclosures). In the damper regions of South Africa, it caused no trouble, but in the dry areas it escaped and spread on its own. It pushed out the natural vegetation, and when the cattle tried to eat this cactus, they received such cuts and wounds that they almost starved. It spread over wide areas and several states, and all efforts to stop it were futile. Then in 1933, the Argentine moth was brought from Australia, where it had been so successful. This was able to stop new growth, killing off the young shoots. But it could not attack the woody base of the older Opuntias. Finally, in 1937, a scale insect was found which could attack the woody parts of the cacti, and so most of the cactus deserts in South Africa have been reclaimed.

Probably nothing is perfect. And while this scale insect did the job on the destructive Opuntias, it also took to eating some special spineless Opuntias that the South Africans were cultivating as cattle fodder, so that it, too, had to be treated with chemical poisons.

But even though the cactus may look like a plant from another world, and behave like a menace from outer space when transplanted from its native America, at home in the mountains and deserts of the New World, little but good can be said of it. Cacti were extremely useful plants to the American Indians and even now they are used to make some of the traditional Indian drinks and dishes that are still popular south of the border.

It was the Opuntias—the plants that caused so much

Cacti in the Southwest

trouble in foreign lands—that were most important to the native Americans. For centuries, during its fruiting season, it was the mainstay of wandering Indian tribes. The Toltecs, and later the Aztecs, both developed a settled agricultural culture and both valued the Opuntia. They planted them near their houses, selecting the species with the biggest and tastiest fruits. Today in Mexico and lands to the south, Opuntia orchards are cultivated and the prickly pear fruit (the best are somewhat larger than a hen's egg) are sold in the markets. The poorer Mexicans go to the hills when they know the Opuntias are in fruit, for there the wild Opuntias provide them with food and drink for the taking.

The fruit of this cactus is made into many different kinds of food. One is a kind of cheese and another is a jam which is spread on the Mexican *tortillas* or flat cakes. In addition, a kind of honey can be prepared, and finally the juice extracted from the fruit is made into an alcoholic drink, a process which probably goes back to the Toltecs. The fruit is also used to improve the taste of the Mexican national drink, *pulque.* This beverage is made from the sap of the agave, a plant related to the cactus. Opuntias bear fruit twice a year and thus seem to provide unending bounty.

The cactus gave the Indians much more than food. It seems unbelievable that these "overgrown thistles" as the Europeans at first thought of them, could produce anything like wood. Yet one of the tree Opuntias, which grows to fifteen or twenty feet high, has thick, flat joints with round stems that grow so hard and tough over the years that they can resist air and moisture for centuries. This wood is used for special purposes such as door sills and for making oars. The tall, columnar cacti also produce good wood for house building and the smaller species with prickly arms are dried in the sun and then used for firewood.

The ingenious Indians found many other uses for the cacti that grew in such variety around them. The stiff hairs of a treelike *Cereus* are made into combs and the long spikes of some of the South American species are sold as knitting needles. The woolly hair of others has been made into fibers for cloth. Certain spines are used as fishhooks and the Indians of lower California extract poison from a cactus for the illegal killing of fish.

Cacti have also brought gifts to the medical profession. The powdered roots of one of the Opuntias are used to make a plaster to set broken bones. Other roots are efficacious against dysentery and some flowers produce a heart stimulant. While these and other medicinal uses go far back in time to pre-Columbian eras, modern medicine is finding useful properties among the cacti. The shoots of the Queen of the Night *(Selenicereus grandiflorus)* and related species are exported to other countries for use in the manufacture of medicines.

And then there is the peyote cactus *(Lophophora williamsii)* which has become famous as a hallucinatory drug. Centuries before Columbus, the Indians had discovered the peculiar properties of this plant and the strange dreams and visions it produces. All kinds of superstitions grew up around it. It was credited with insuring long life, good health, rain when needed and a good harvest! It was made a part of many Indian religious rites and the later Christian priests tried to stamp them out. In the end, they had to let the Indians

Saguaro in bloom

continue their peyote cults along with the new Christian religion.

Whether we consider the usefulness of the cactus at home or the problems it has caused when transplanted abroad, nobody can dispute the beauty and distinction that it lends to our desert regions.

The giant saguaro produces its flowers at the top of the trunk, where only birds and insects can reach them. This cactus provides a home for many desert creatures. The woodpecker makes its nest in the trunk, and that nest may be later taken over by the little elf owl of our southwestern deserts. The bushy, thornier cacti in turn provide a safe nesting place for the desert wren. She can squeeze in between the spikes that would discourage a predator.

The smaller species of cactus are fascinating to study. Whether you make a cactus garden outdoors or indoors, there is a wealth of strange forms and shapes to choose from. And while they may appear rough, spiny and ugly at first, when they bloom they put forth brilliant flowers, usually red or yellow. In the desert these are pollinated by desert insects and hummingbirds. There are also night-flowering species that have white flowers and are pollinated by moths and bats.

The giant saguaro and the organ pipe cacti are both so extraordinary that sanctuaries have been established to preserve the more spectacular of the groves. A trip to one of these national monuments in Arizona can be the high point of a vacation. The towering arms of these mighty plants, seen against a desert sunset, are unforgettable.

10

Rabbit Reckoning

Like many of the creatures that have accompanied the human species as we spread around the globe, the rabbit was originally native to one fairly small area—in this case believed to be the Iberian peninsula. Excavations indicate that it was restricted to this region by the last ice age. This is the European rabbit (*Oryctolagus cuniculus*), made famous by the authors of such books as *Peter Rabbit* and more recently, *Watership Down.* It is not the same species as the North American rabbit (*Sylvilagus floridanus*) which does not burrow and is not so much of a pest.

The European rabbit likes open spaces and is gregarious in its habits; quite different from the American rabbit, which is a woodland species and leads a more solitary life. The European rabbit lives in large colonies, called warrens, where it digs complicated tunnels. The various domestic breeds of rabbits come from this wild stock. Although it may seem that rabbits relish the choicest plants in the garden, they can also eat a wide variety of tough grasses and leaves. Cattle and sheep, known as ruminants, take care of this problem by

Rabbit gardens, from old French drawings

digesting their rough fodder twice. They chew and swallow it quickly while eating, and later they sit around and regurgitate the partially digested food and chew it again. This is called chewing the cud. Rabbits accomplish the same result in a slightly different way. When they go back into their burrows after eating, they pass soft pellets. Each rabbit eats its own pellets, and in this way the food is digested twice. Only when they are outside do they discharge the typical hard droppings of rabbits.

When the female is pregnant, she digs a special burrow of her own which she lines with leaves and fur from her body. Here she gives birth to five or more babies which are born naked, deaf and blind, and weigh only a little more than an ounce. They grow quickly and the female mates again twelve hours after her litter is born. In this way she can have more than one litter in a season, which accounts for how rabbits can multiply very quickly.

The Romans were the first to appreciate the benefits of *O.*

cuniculus, although the Phoenicians had made note of these strange little beasts when they sailed past Iberia around 1100 B.C. As the Roman armies moved around the Mediterranean Sea, they took the rabbit with them. At that time, the animal was not domesticated as we know it today. The Romans were already raising the hare as a source of food and they treated the rabbit in the same way. The animals were caught in the wild and kept in large "gardens," surrounded by a solid wall. Inside were all kinds of plants to furnish food and shelter for the captives. This worked fairly well with the hares, but when rabbits were added there were complications. The two species are not compatible and the smaller rabbits usually won out. Furthermore, since the rabbits are burrowers, they could dig their way out of the "gardens," and the walls had to be extended below ground in order to prevent this. Still, the Romans enjoyed eating rabbit, and so they took them with them. And as a few rabbits always escaped, the species was soon living and breeding in most Mediterranean countries.

After the fall of the Roman Empire, the succeeding barbarian rulers continued the custom of rabbit garden culture, perhaps not so much for food as for the pleasure of hunting small game near home. Rabbits were preferred to hares because, while the latter will not breed in captivity, the rabbits quickly increased their numbers. This practice gradually spread throughout Europe, and a French manuscript of 1393 shows ladies hunting rabbits in a rabbit garden with bows and arrows, clubs and dogs. At this time, the idea of keeping the rabbits on an island—thus dispensing with the garden walls—developed, and Queen Elizabeth of England in the sixteenth century had a rabbit island.

This method of keeping rabbits did not lead to domestication. The rabbits bred as they pleased, and since the hunters took the least wary, natural selection operated to breed for wildness. The actual domestication of the rabbit was accomplished by the mediaeval monks. During Lent, all Christians were supposed to give up the eating of meat. Fish is considered a proper substitute, but the monks often did not have fish, and so they developed the theory that the unborn or newly born offspring of the rabbit was not really meat. They called them *laurices* and they became a favorite lenten dish. And so, in order to obtain these newly born rabbits, the does (females) were taken into the monasteries, and little by little rabbits were raised in a domestic state. As early as the year 590, Bishop Gregory of Tours was inveighing against this Lenten habit of eating rabbit fetuses, but his words seem to have carried little weight. By 1149, an abbot in Germany was asking a French abbot to send him two pairs of rabbits. And by the middle of the sixteenth century, the famous writer, Agricola, was describing black, white and piebald rabbits—an indication of how far breeding for certain strains had progressed. The first picture of a white rabbit was painted by Titian in 1530. Called the *Madonna with the Rabbit*, the painting hangs in the Louvre.

These domestic rabbits of the monks spread across Europe some 300 years ahead of the wild rabbits. The latter were the result of escapes from the rabbit gardens—the property of the nobility. Then, too, the European rabbit does not like forests or even high grass. It seeks out fields and open country. As long as there were great forests all over Europe, the few escapees did not increase their numbers. But as Europe developed into farming country, the rabbits could multiply and expand their population.

By the mid-seventeenth century, the English had taken up rabbit breeding. Now the animals began to be valued for their fur as well as for their flesh. And the Angora, or long-haired rabbit, made its appearance around 1723. At this time also, many of the European nations were busy sailing the oceans of the world and building foreign empires wherever they could. Portuguese sailors formed a habit of depositing rabbits and goats on desolate islands, the idea being that if shipwrecked sailors should land there, they would find something to eat. But the plan was not always a happy one. The animals destroyed the native fauna and flora and often ate themselves out of existence. This was only the beginning of the long, bleak history of transplanted rabbits.

Rabbits are soft, cuddly creatures and evoke a sympathetic feeling in people—unless they happen to be raiding the garden! They are also very good eating and provide many

European wild rabbit

happy hours for the hunter. Wild rabbits became numerous in England between the sixteenth century (when they were kept in rabbit gardens) and the eighteenth century, by which time the escapees had made themselves at home and built up their numbers. And however much the farmers might protest their depredations, to the average Englishman they seemed a part of the home landscape.

The first English settlers in Australia took rabbits with them, for rabbits can endure the hardships of a long sea voyage better than almost any other domestic animal. However, these were domestic rabbits, bred for many generations in captivity. They were used for food and if there were any escapees, they did not survive in the harsh Australian bush.

Then in the mid-nineteenth century, a man called Thomas Austin decided that he wanted to live like an English squire. And shooting rabbits is one of the pleasures of being gentry in rural England. Moreover, Austin missed the cute little bunnies in this land of the kangaroo. He owned a large estate near Melbourne and he sent to England for rabbits to populate it. Domesticated rabbits would not be tough enough for the Australian wilds, so he insisted on the wild rabbits from the English countryside—a dozen of each sex. They arrived by ship in 1859, and some people have remarked that the name of the clipper ship—*Lightning*—was prophetic. For in a remarkably short time, it seemed that a bolt of ecological lightning had struck the continent of Australia.

The rabbits had no trouble in adjusting to their new environment. There was plenty of vegetation for food and a climate that allowed them to breed all year around. And there were no predators. There was nothing to stop them from multiplying at the phenomenal rate that rabbits can multiply.

Within six years, Thomas Austin and his hunting friends had shot and trapped 20,000 rabbits—but there were still 10,000 left, and they were spreading far outside the borders of his estate.

The Australians began control measures early, but they had little effect. A bounty was put on rabbit tails. Some government agencies began to construct rabbit-proof fences. During the 1880s, the state of Victoria paid out 350,000 pounds for bounties and fences. And New South Wales and South Australia expended four times as much. But the rabbits continued to increase and to spread across the land. In this favorable climate, a doe could have six litters a year and there are often six bunnies to a litter.

Rabbits have a fondness for the best vegetation in the garden. They also like the sweetest grass, clover, alfalfa and the best pasture grasses. But they will also eat oak seedlings and cactus and they nibble the plants so close to the ground that vegetation cannot recover. Nine rabbits are said to consume the forage of two fine sheep. And sheep were Australia's most important crop. Not only were the rabbits taking the food from the ranchers' animals, they were turning the countryside into a wasteland. The rabbits are estimated to have reached a population of two billion—three hundred times the human population of the continent.

Since shooting, trapping and poison did not do the trick, and fences were always having to be extended (for if one pregnant female managed to squeeze through or dig under, the usefulness of the fence was gone), the Australians decided to import predators. The fox is the natural predator of the rabbit in Europe, so foxes were brought from England. Unfortunately, when the foxes were released on these vast sheep farms, they developed a taste for lamb and paid little attention to the rabbits. Other predators were tried: ferrets, weasels, even mongooses. They turned to raiding poultry yards and made hardly a dent on the rabbit millions.

The frantic Australians tried digging up the burrows—an impossible job, as the warrens can be eight feet deep. Strychnine was poured into waterholes, but the sheep suffered more than the rabbits did. Poison gas was pumped into rabbit holes, but while thousands died, some always escaped to start the population exploding once more. In 1887, the government offered a reward of 25,000 pounds for any method of "effective extermination" of the rabbits. Nobody earned it. Australia's grazing lands were being damaged to a tune of $60 million a year.

In an effort to recoup some of its losses, Australia began to export frozen rabbit meat. It also built up an industry on rabbit skins. The hair is used to make felt for hats. And because of a superstition that says that luck clings to the left hind foot of a rabbit caught in a graveyard in the dark of the moon—several million rabbit feet are sold in the United States yearly.

All these rabbit industries only made up a fraction of the loss to Australian agriculture. But help finally came in the guise of a deadly rabbit disease. *Myxomatosis* was first discovered in 1897, when the white laboratory rabbits of a South American scientist caught this disease, common to the wild rabbits of that continent, and promptly died. But it was not until 1927 that another South American biologist, reading the earlier record, had a bright idea. Since all laboratory rabbits are descended from the European wild rabbit, the disease should be equally lethal to the pests in Australia. But it was not as easy as it seemed. Experiments were made. Animals inoculated with the virus in the laboratory always died, but the disease failed to infect the wild populations. What was wrong?

The scientists persisted through one discouragement after another. It was not until the 1950s that the answer was found. Like malaria in man, the disease must be spread by a vector! The vectors for myxomatosis include mosquitoes, blackflies, lice and rabbit fleas. When infected rabbits were introduced into a population living along a river, with lots of biting insects

Rabbits in Australia—before 1950

in the area, an epidemic resulted and the rabbit population was quickly wiped out. Once this was known, the proper methods were introduced and in three years Australia's rabbit population was reduced by 96 percent. Wool production increased by $50 million a year.

The disease was also introduced into France and England by long suffering agriculturists. Rabbits were reduced to a minimum in both countries, and there were loud cries of protest from the felt hat industry, which came near being wiped out. Some hunters and furriers even wanted to sue the scientists for damages! But scientists doubt that all European rabbits will be exterminated. This species has a remarkable ability to survive and there are always some left after every epidemic. As the housefly has developed an immunity to DDT, the rabbit may in time develop one to myxomatosis. When that happens, humans had better watch out!

You might think that people would have learned something from the dire example of Australia, but such is seldom the case. In the year 1900, a lighthouse keeper on Smith's Island, one of the San Juan Islands in Puget Sound, decided that he would like to keep rabbits. It would give him something to do in his solitude and he could sell the meat in Seattle. His were domestic rabbits, and he kept them in cages and there was no problem until he was transferred elsewhere and another keeper came to watch over Smith's Island. For some reason, the first man did not take his rabbits away with him, and as the new keeper had no interest in rabbits, he simply turned them loose.

The U.S. Navy maintained a radio compass station on Smith's Island, and during the following years the small staff operating the station watched the increasing rabbit population with some alarm. By 1924, the rabbits had almost denuded the island of vegetation and most of the birds that once nested there had deserted the barren spot. What's more, the Navy's buildings were leaning and tilting at odd angles, being slowly undermined by the extensive rabbit warrens. The Navy called in the Biological Survey, which sent two scientists to cope with the problem. By means of poison and gas, they were able to exterminate most of this rabbit population. Since the animals were on an island, they could not spread farther afield. However, a few rabbits escaped the slaughter, so that there are still rabbits on the San Juan Islands. And in the 1950s, some hunting clubs in the eastern states ordered rabbits from there and released them in the woods of Ohio, Pennsylvania, Illinois and other states. When they were threatened with prosecution under the Lacey Act, which forbids the importation of any foreign wild animal without permission from the Department of Agriculture, the sportsmen pointed out that the rabbits were not foreign, but originated in another part of the United States.

Fortunately, no rabbit population explosion has resulted. But it seems that some people just like to live dangerously. Or is it that they don't consider the consequences of their acts?

V

HAPPY EXCEPTIONS

11

Pheasant Fantasy

Lest you think that all importations of foreign wildlife turn out to be disasters, we will tell the stories of a very few that have brought blessings with them. But we must emphasize that these are a mere fraction of the many plants and animals that are brought into our country to take their chances here and perhaps to wreak havoc among our native animals or to cause confusion to our way of life.

Foremost among the happy ventures is the ring-necked pheasant (*Phasianus colchicus torquatus*). Pheasants are gallinaceous birds, a group that includes wild turkeys, grouse, quail and the jungle fowl from which our barnyard chickens are descended. The pheasants and the fowl are both Asiatic in origin, but unlike the chicken, the pheasant has never become completely domesticated.

Early peoples of hunting cultures appreciated the pheasant as much as our hunters do today, and there is a story that Jason brought it back to Greece from the Caucasus region, along with Medea and the famous golden fleece. However, it seems likely that the bird slowly filtered into the Mediterranean region in the trade between the two areas. Later, the Romans took it to all parts of the Ancient World. They ate both the eggs and the birds, and with them it arrived in England.

Through the centuries, the English enjoyed pheasant hunting, in early times with bow and arrow and later with the gun. So when they began to colonize the New World, they were disappointed that there was no bird here to compare with the pheasant. True, we had wild turkeys and quail and grouse and, until we killed them all, the passenger pigeon. But for hunting sport there is nothing like the rise of a startled pheasant from under your feet!

There were many early attempts to introduce the pheasant to America. Even before George Washington was born, some pheasants were released in the colonies and the governor of New York brought a dozen of the birds to what is now Governor's Island. Later, Richard Bache, who was Benjamin Franklin's son-in-law, released some pheasants on his estate in New Jersey. But none of these implantations "took." The birds did not increase their numbers. In fact, in most cases, they simply disappeared. It seemed that the pheasant could not establish a home in the New World.

Nowadays, when we see pheasants everywhere—well, *almost* everywhere, in at least eighteen of the fifty states—it is hard to understand the many failures. And when success did come, it was at the other side of the continent and with the Chinese branch of the pheasant family, which is why our birds have the white ring around the neck and the English pheasants do not.

There are a number of different races of pheasants, all closely enough related to interbreed. The Chinese pheasant (*P. torquatus*) found in eastern Asia; and the western, Caucasian type (*P. colchicus*) which does not have the neck ring and which has spread to England and points between. There is also a green pheasant in Japan (*P. versicolor*). At one time they were considered distinct species, but today they are recognized as one species with several subspecies. Our American brand of pheasant is really a hybrid, having blood and genes from all three types.

The man who had the first success with importing the pheasant to North America was Judge Owen N. Denny and he lived in Portland, Oregon. In the 1880s, he was sent to China in the consular service and while there became enamored of the beautiful birds of that country. How wonderful it would be to have a bird like the pheasant running about the home

Ring-Neck pheasant

woods during the hunting season! His first effort, when he sent sixty Mongolian pheasants in little wicker baskets by ship to Oregon, was a failure. That was in 1881. The passage was a rough one and the birds arrived in poor condition. They were turned loose as the Judge instructed, but before long they had all disappeared. The effort had cost him $300, along with other plants and birds that had been in the shipment and none of which survived.

But Judge Denny tried again the next year, and this time he had a large wicker cage constructed in the hold of the ship, with gravel on the floor and potted plants, so that the birds could move about and feel at home. And this time his luck held. The voyage was more peaceful and the ten cocks and eighteen hens arrived safely in Portland. When they were released behind the old Denny home on Peterson Butte, they made themselves right at home. By the time Denny returned in 1884, they were spreading out all over the county, and ten years after their introduction, Oregon had its first open season on pheasants. This was a "first" for the country—in fact, for the hemisphere, and 50,000 birds were taken in that first season without endangering the population. The pheasant was established in America!

The pheasant is a beautiful bird to look at, and extremely good to eat. The cock has the brilliant plumage and long spotted tail. The hen is more drably colored, for she must sit on the nest and her feathers are well camouflaged to blend with the leaves and grasses. The cock gathers a harem of hens, for which he must often fight off the other cocks. Harems may be as large as eighteen, and in experimental breeding it has been found that one cock can handle as many as fifty hens! But it is doubtful that one cock could round up that many in the wild.

Battles between the cocks may begin as early as February and by May nesting is well under way. The hens nest on the ground, scraping a little hollow and lining it with grass and weeds. Each hen lays around a dozen eggs and sits motionless on them, and her mottled brown coloring helps to hide her from the eyes of any predator. The cock takes no responsibility for his hens or their eggs, and leaves the twenty-three-day incubation entirely up to her. Both wild and domestic animals may destroy the eggs before they can hatch. Snakes, skunks, cats and dogs take their toll. But once the eggs hatch the little ones can run from danger. The chicks are precocial. That is, they belong to the type of bird that can run and find its food as soon as it is hatched. No waiting in the nest to be fed! An hour after hatching, the pheasant chicks, which weigh less than an ounce, are running about, pecking at insects, and obeying their mother's clucking instructions.

Other states in the Union were not slow in trying to emulate Oregon's success with the pheasant. In fact, almost every state had to try, but not all of them were successful. Of the forty-eight continental states that tried to get into the pheasant business, only eighteen were successful. Foremost of these was South Dakota, and they did it with a minimum of expense and effort. Why? Because the terrain and the climate were suitable for the bird. No studies were made on these problems in the beginning, and states poured thousands of dollars into the buying and rearing of pheasants, only to have the efforts come to nothing.

Since then, scientists have done research on the life and requirements of the pheasant, but even so the reasons for failure often remain obscure. In their native Asia, pheasants can adapt to a wide variety of habitat. They can live at sea level and at an 8,000-foot altitude. They can endure the heat of the Imperial Valley in California. They seem to do best, however, in cultivated areas, where they can be seen running along roadways or through grain fields. But for some reason it seems that they cannot live in our southeastern states.

Hundreds of thousands of dollars have been spent by wildlife enthusiasts in these states in a vain effort to cultivate the birds, and as recently as 1950, Kentucky released 20,000 pheasants over eight years. But the birds were unable to establish a breeding population. The noted naturalist, Aldo Leopold, observed in 1930 that pheasants seemed to range no further south than the limits of the last glaciers. He suggested that the calcium content of the soil might have a bearing on the pheasants' eggs. Later experiments confirmed this. A calcium-deficient diet does not lead to success in hatching pheasant eggs. Another suggestion was that high temperatures may cut down on hatchability, and experiments also confirmed this theory. Then how account for the success of pheasants in the hot Imperial Valley? The only answer is that there the heat is very dry.

Today, South Dakota advertises itself as the top pheasant state in the Union. Some three million ring-necks are shot there annually without reducing the pheasant population. But a place that runs it a close second for pheasant hunting is a small island in a corner of Lake Erie, belonging to Ontario, Canada. This island, Pelee, lies twenty miles across the lake from Ohio, one of the lucky states that has been successful in establishing the pheasant.

It turned out that Ohio wanted some bass for its fisheries and Ontario wanted pheasants for Pelee, so a swap was arranged. One hundred bass for one hundred pheasants, and a game warden from Ohio set out to take the pheasants to Pelee.

"I'd never heard of the place," he told people later.

But he took two crates of young birds by truck to Lake

Pheasant chick—one hour old

Erie, where he boarded a boat belonging to the state of Ohio. At the island's dock, they were met by an old market wagon, pulled by an aging gray horse. While the Canadian drove the wagon around the island, the American stood up and tossed out pheasants, two at a time. Then they went back to the dock, where the American loaded four milk cans into the boat. They contained the 100 bass, and all the way across the lake, he dipped them in fresh lake water to keep them in good condition.

The whole operation was hush-hush at the time, because the Ohio authorities feared that the state's hunters would protest if they knew that their prized pheasants were being swapped for fish. But the trade turned out to be successful for both sides. Not a pheasant or a fish was lost in transit. Some years later, the American was invited to come back to Pelee to sample the pheasant hunting. What he saw was unbelievable.

"There were pheasants everywhere," he said. "You had to get out and chase them out of the road."

At first the farmers on Pelee had objected to the new birds, which made inroads on their grain. But soon they found that the ring-necks were an economic asset. Now they rent lodgings to thousands of hunters who come during the fall season. And all that was paid for this bonanza was 100 fish.

12

Fisherman's Delight

Another creature that has been successfully transplanted around the world is a fish. You might think that fish would be the hardest of all creatures to move long distances, since they must have water of the right consistency and temperature, and a hundred years ago, when this work was first attempted, there were no airplanes to move the precious cargo in a day or two. Long sea voyages were required, and the British, who were the chief movers, wanted their fish on the other side of the world, in the newly settled lands of Australia and New Zealand.

The fish involved was the brown trout (*Salmo fario*) a native of the streams of Europe, Algeria and a corner of Asia. For centuries Englishmen have enjoyed battling this game fish in the streams and rivers of England, and when they went to live in the other hemisphere, they missed that exciting sport.

The brown trout is mottled olive green, brown and yellow and usually weighs from eight to twelve pounds, but big ones can come much heavier. It is a wary fish and takes all the fisherman's skill to hook and can put up a good fight before it is hauled ashore. It is also very good eating.

These virtues made it seem imperative that it should be imported to the new colonies, and as early as 1851 efforts were made to transport the eggs. But the first attempts failed, due to inexperience, rough weather and lack of ice. Good fishermen are not easily discouraged, and in 1864 the first shipment of trout eggs reached Tasmania, an island just south of Australia. Three hundred of them hatched in the fishery there and began the propagation of brown trout in that part of the world.

New Zealand had a more difficult time. The first shipment of eggs destined for that country all died at sea, because a careless sailor dropped a lump of white lead putty into the container. Discouraged by this, the New Zealanders turned to the successful fishery in Tasmania for their trout. It would be a shorter and quicker voyage across the southern sea. But still they were plagued with bad luck. Of 800 eggs purchased, only three hatched in the New Zealand fishery. Hoping that both sexes might be represented, the fishermen prepared a pond for the little fish in the gardens of the Canterbury Acclimatization Society, but before the fish could be installed, one of them was lost. Now there was a fifty-fifty chance that there might

Brown trout

be one fish of each sex and the New Zealanders waited hopefully to find out. However, the fish had no time to grow bigger before a tremendous flood completely inundated the gardens, and the fry were swept into a swamp. Considering the New Zealanders' run of luck, this should have been the end of the brown trout. But fortunately, before the flood, the fish fanciers had built a spawning raceway and somehow the two fish made their way to it. Against all expectations, the little fish turned out to be male and female and within a few years they were producing enough trout eggs to stock the streams of New Zealand and assure its reputation as one of the best trout fishing countries in the world.

In the northern hemisphere, the brown trout begins its spawning run in November and December. The females swim up the streams and lay their eggs in nests they hollow out of the gravel in the bed of the stream. There the male fertilizes them. The female may lay anywhere from 200 to 6,000 eggs, depending on her age and size. It takes these trout four to six years to become adult and the water in the stream must stay at 51° F. in order to hatch the eggs. Hatching takes between forty-eight and fifty-two days.

Following the success of the Tasmanians, trout eggs were shipped to many countries around the world. All that was required was a flowing stream with clean water and the right temperature. For instance, Chile has made its Rio Calcurrupe in the high Andes into one of the best trout streams.

So it was natural that Americans should want to get into the game of brown trout importing. The first to do so was a German who dispatched a shipment of trout eggs from Germany to New York in 1882. These were cared for in the state hatchery and in the spring the fry were released in the Pere Marquette River in Michigan. A year later, more trout were imported, this time from Loch Leven in Scotland. For some years there was an argument about the two kinds of brown trout, the Scotch and the German. But today it is realized that they are one and the same species. They all adapted equally well to North American waters, and most streams that are clean enough and cold enough have brown trout in them today.

Some American fishermen do not like the brown trout,

saying that they destroy rainbow and brook trout, which are much easier to catch. An angler who spends a short vacation on a brown trout stream and catches nothing may be resentful. But the expert, who likes to match his wits against the wariest fish in the stream, has nothing but praise for the alien brown trout.

A second case of fish moving concerns a saltwater fish. This one was not moved across an ocean but across a continent. *Roccus saxatilis*, the striped bass, is a native of the Atlantic Ocean. It brings wealth and happiness to the fishermen of our eastern seaboard, but there was no such fish along the Pacific coast. S. R. Throckmorton, chairman of the California Fish Commission, did not think this was fair. And when he considered the recent building of the transcontinental railroad, he decided that he could do something about it.

In this case, the fish themselves were transported. In 1897, a tank of year-old bass arrived in San Francisco and the fish were promptly dumped into San Francisco Bay. Two years later, the çommissioner tried again. Altogether, 435 striped bass were brought from the Atlantic coast and dumped into the Pacific Ocean. And they flourished. They multiplied fantastically. Within ten years, striped bass were being sold in the California fish markets. Within twenty years, the commercial catch reached over a million pounds a year.

Sport fishermen, however, did not like to have their fish

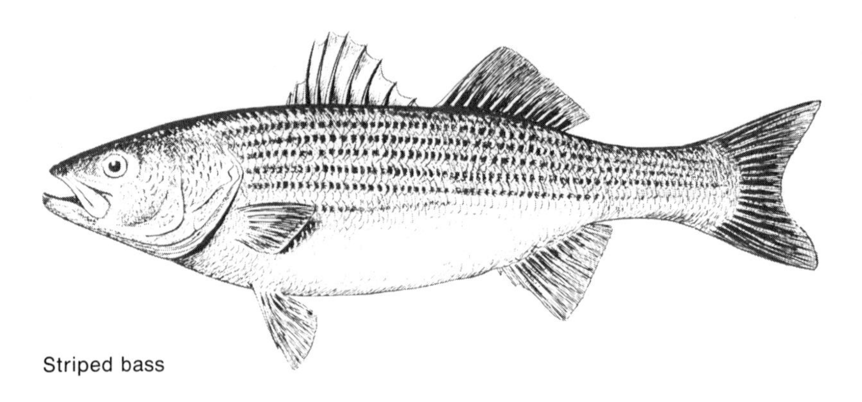

Striped bass

depleted by commercial fishing and in 1935 the striped bass became a protected game fish. In the San Francisco Bay area, it is now abundant and is considered the primary game fish. It has spread north in smaller numbers as far as the Columbia River and southward toward Los Angeles.

The striped bass grows to be a large fish. It is greenish blue above and white beneath, with six or seven rows of dark spots along the sides. It generally runs twelve to twenty pounds, but a fifty pounder is not unusual. Like the brown trout, it tests the ability of the fisherman. It is swift and strong, dashing through the surf and challenging the angler who tries to pull it ashore.

The male bass takes three years to mature and the female four. A seventy-five- pound female is believed to lay as many as 10 million eggs in a single season. The adults move up the streams in spring and back out to sea in late summer. The eggs are laid in the water and sink so slowly that they may drift and float until they hatch. Hatching takes place in seventy-four hours if the water is 58° F., and in less time when the water is warmer. The fry stay in the streams until they are two years old, when they form schools and make distant migrations. They are long-lived fish. A striped bass at the New York Aquarium lived for twenty-three years.

In the Atlantic, the striped bass is found from Nova Scotia to Florida, but their spawning streams are located from New Jersey to South Carolina. In the present century, there have been many dams built on streams in this area, and an unexpected development arose in connection with the fish.

When, in 1941, the gates were closed on the new Pinopolis Dam at Moncks Corner, South Carolina, it interrupted the yearly spawning run of striped bass up the Santee and Cooper rivers. The waters impounded by the dam formed two large lakes, called Marion and Moultrie, which supply electric power to a large area. Nobody was surprised when bass were seen in the waters below the dam. But when after a while striped bass began to turn up in the two lakes above, it was cause for comment. It was presumed that some bass had been locked in above the dam when it was closed. But as the fishing in Lakes Marion and Moultrie got better and better, biologists began to wonder. Could the striped bass be going through its entire life cycle in these freshwater lakes far from the sea? Such a thing was unheard of, but tests soon proved it to be so. Fishing in the new lakes became famous, and fishermen rushed there from all over the country to try their luck at landing the big bass.

This unusual development has made fish experts dream and experiment. Perhaps the bass could be planted in inland waters, far from their native ocean. Fish experts from such states as Arkansas, Kentucky and Oklahoma began to consider their lakes as possible homes for *R. saxatilis*. But the bass is after all a saltwater fish, and many of these experiments failed. Still, the bass has been introduced into the Kerr Reservoir, the thirty-nine-mile-long body of water on the Virginia–North Carolina border formed by damming the Roanoke River. This river was another of the historic spawning grounds of the striped bass, and when young fry were introduced there, they prospered.

Perhaps there is something in the water of their ancestral rivers that makes it possible for the bass to live there without returning to the ocean. Perhaps that something is missing in the waters of the mid-continent lakes. Whatever it is, scientists are studying the unexpected behavior of the striped bass, and when they find the answer, this wonderful fish may be spread to even more places around the country.

13

Caribou and Reindeer Are Cousins

At Christmastime we appreciate the magic of Santa Claus' reindeer, flying through the air and landing with gift-laden sleigh upon the roof. But few people realize that there are just as many remarkable facts about the reindeer as there are myths and legends.

Reindeer and caribou are the same species of deer (*Rangifer tarandus*), the distinction being that the reindeer has been domesticated and the caribou has not. *R. tarandus* inhabits the entire north circumpolar region, from Siberia through Scandinavia, Greenland and Canada to Alaska. There are numerous subspecies recognized, such as the forest caribou, the tundra reindeer, the barren lands caribou; each has its scientific name, made by adding a third name to *Rangifer tarandus* (or *R. tarandus arcticus*, the North American tundra reindeer). But fundamentally, they are all the same animal. The chief difference is that the Old World animals have experienced thousands of years of semidomestication, whereas those in the New World—where the native peoples, Eskimos and Indians, remained hunting peoples—are still completely wild.

The reindeer is an animal of the Ice Age. The mammoth, the woolly rhinoceros, the giant cave bear are all gone. But the reindeer survives in what is probably an interglacial period. It is built to live in ice and snow, from its sharp, splayed hooves, adapted to cutting through ice and walking on snow, to its heavy, waterproof coat. The hairs are hollow and filled with air, giving a buoyant quality, helpful when the animal has to swim a river. Even the nose is well protected with fur. It is believed that the reindeer evolved originally in America and then spread into all the circumpolar regions. It has practically no northern limits and is the only member of the deer family in which both sexes have antlers.

One of the most remarkable things about the reindeer is its diet. Its chief food is lichen, sometimes called reindeer moss, which carpets the summer northlands. But it also eats other plants, such as willow, and it is especially fond of mushrooms. Reindeer eat even the poisonous varieties of these fungi, and when they do, they lapse into a drowsy state, making it easy to capture them.

Most animals like the reindeer—cattle, horses, other deer—are strictly herbivorous and will eat only vegetable matter. But the reindeer will also eat fish. They will even eat meat, if necessary, and scientists have theorized that perhaps this trait helped in their domestication. Perhaps in early times they scavenged the camps of hunters much as the wolves did before they became dogs.

These deer are even said to capture and eat lemmings, those little mouselike creatures that sometimes become so numerous in the northlands that they are almost a pest. Some experts have an interesting explanation for this undeerlike behavior. For in addition to all these idiosyncracies, the reindeer have a passion for salt, which leads them to drink seawater, eat seaweed, and finally to drink urine! Hunters use urine as a lure to trap the animals. The theory about the lemmings is that when they are grabbed by a reindeer, they urinate in fear and this makes them a tasty morsel to the big animal. However, J. G. Doherty, curator of mammals at the New York Zoological Society, suggests that it may be a deficiency of protein in their diet that causes the reindeer to eat fish and lemmings.

Caribou migrating

Reindeer are very gregarious. Much more so than other species of deer. It is rare to see a single reindeer. Herds are smaller in the forests, ranging from a few deer to several hundred. But on the tundra, they number in the tens of thousands, especially at migration time, when several herds may merge as they travel the well-worn routes. One observer, as recently as 1917, describes "a clear view of ten miles each way and it was one army of caribou." Such a herd may number in the millions.

Why do the caribou and reindeer migrate for hundreds of miles? One reason is that they cannot stand warm weather. Anything above 50° F. is too warm for them. In the fall, the herds come down from the tundra to spend the winter in the protection of the forest fringes. But as soon as spring comes, they start to move north. They go to feed on the summer pastures of lichen on the vast tundra. But they also try to escape the hordes of mosquitoes which infest the northern lands in the summer. In the spring, the does give birth to their fawns, and the migration is in search of a cold climate in the Arctic lands where the babies will not be harassed by these bloodsucking insects.

It was this migratory habit that made the reindeer the mainstay of many early peoples in the Paleolithic and later ages. In the glacial periods, early men learned to recognize the migration routes of the reindeer and caribou. They knew that if they went to a certain place at a certain time of year, they would find thousands of these animals passing through and that it would be easy to kill a number of them. And aside from the food which a large reindeer supplied, the hides made excellent winter clothing and the sinews made the best of thread. Even today it is preferred for sewing boots and canoes of reindeer hide, for the sinew expands when wet and seals the holes. Knife handles and needles are still made from the antlers.

The reindeer had a direct effect upon the arts of those early days. In many of the French and Spanish caves, where artists of 30,000 years ago left their paintings, reindeer have an important place. Reindeer horns were also used for carving by the early hunters, and beautiful horn sculptures have been dug up at a Swiss site: reindeer carved upon reindeer antlers.

At what point did the reindeer become domesticated? The matter has not been settled to everybody's satisfaction. It used to be thought to have happened rather late in the history of domestication. But some experts now think that it was one of the first animals to have felt the yoke of man. It is easy to see how early hunters, who made a practice of lying in wait for the herds on their annual migration, might take up the practice of following along, so that they would have their food always near at hand. In doing this, they were doing what the wolves still do to this day: migrating with the migration. And when the wolf had been brought under control and become a dog, to help in hunting the reindeer, the next step would be for the dogs to help men control the herds.

The eminent authority, F. E. Zeuner, thinks that the reindeer may have been the second animal to be domesticated. He divides that process into two parts. In the first part, certain cultural practices were developed. Male fawns were castrated by biting; the ears of the deer were notched to identify ownership; the lasso was invented to capture them; and salt or urine was used to attract the animals. Much later, when these northern nomadic tribes came into contact with settled agricultural people who had cattle, they learned from them how to milk their animals, how to ride them and how to use them to pull sledges.

The dates for these events are still open to question. But Zeuner cites the interesting case of the frozen horses that were dug up from some Scythian mound burials in the Altai Mountains of Mongolia. One of the horses wears a reindeer mask; The burial is placed in the fifth century B.C.

Whatever the date of the domestication of the reindeer, its

Reindeer swimming across fjord

history is certainly very different from that of the horse or the cow. Those animals have led a fairly stationary life, with a barn or a stable to return to at the end of the day. But the reindeer still lives its wild existence in snow and wind, still wandering from north to south and back again. Only now its owners wander with it. It gives life and sustenance to many northern tribes throughout the Old World, such as the Tungus of eastern Siberia and the Samoyed of northern Siberia. Each of these has its own way of cultural nomadism. Some may ride the animals and some may not. Some may use it as a draft animal and some may not. But all have built their lives around this remarkable beast.

One of the few remaining modern peoples to live by the reindeer are the Lapps. Their herds total around 575,000 animals, spread across Norway, Sweden and Finland. George Kent, who visited the Lapps, wrote about his experiences for the *Reader's Digest.* He says that the animals are usually surly, resentful of domestication. To milk a reindeer doe, the Lapps must first tie her up, and they get little more than half a teacup per milking. But reindeer milk has four times the butterfat of cow's milk. The Lapps freeze it and drop it into their coffee as we drop sugar cubes.

Mr. Kent took a ride in a *pulkha*, the Lapland sleigh, against the better judgment of his hosts. A reindeer can run up to forty-five miles an hour and has a will of its own. He says it was a hair-raising experience, for the deer was running wild and its hoofs showered him with pellets of ice and snow.

In the New World, the caribou has not been domesticated. The people native to this hemisphere, the Indians and the Eskimos, continued to be hunters. They know when the caribou will migrate north and south and what routes they will take, and they go there to make a killing. But they do not follow the herds and they have never developed the arts of nomadism and domestication. There have been times when the big herds have changed their migration routes, and Eskimo or Indian villages have almost starved.

Because of this, some well-meaning persons about a hundred years ago got the idea that it would be helpful to these northern people if they could have domestic reindeer instead of their wild caribou. The reindeer, with its many thousands of years as a domestic animal, would be easier to handle than the wild caribou, which has never felt the hand of man. Dr. Sheldon Jackson, a missionary, was alarmed in 1891 at the way the Alaskan Eskimos were dying of starvation. He observed that their relatives, only fifty-six miles away across the Bering Strait, seemed always to be well fed. He decided that the difference was reindeer, and he petitioned the United States government to import some. At first, Congress refused. But when Dr. Jackson raised $2,000 and brought over 187 of the animals himself, and when these seemed to be doing well, the government relented and imported another 1,100 reindeer to Alaska.

That was the beginning of a reindeer experiment that has had its ups and downs and is still going on. At first, the reindeer did well, and by the year 1931, there were 500,000 in Alaska. Herding reindeer became big business. Reindeer meat was frozen and shipped to markets around the country. But in 1937, the government decided that the reindeer had been imported for the benefit of the Eskimos and should not be used to make outsiders rich. They bought up all the animals in private hands and gave them to the Eskimos to manage. Now Eskimos are fundamentally a hunting people. They do not have behind them the traditions of thousands of years of nomadic management of reindeer herds, as do the natives of Siberia and Scandinavia. They did not take proper care of their herds, and used them only when they wanted to slaughter them. In a very short time the large herds had dwindled to almost nothing.

One should not blame the Alaskan Eskimos for what happened to their reindeer herds. They could no more turn into counterparts of the Lapp reindeer herders in one generation than the wild caribou could turn into the domesticated reindeer. And there are more angles to the problem than the matter of reindeer culture. When the herds had dwindled to 19,000 by 1952, the Department of the Interior sent experts to help the Eskimos. They found that there are many forces at work that make for success or disaster in reindeer herding.

In 1911, for instance, 40 reindeer were taken to the Pribilof Islands to supply the residents with fresh meat. Two islands were involved, St. Paul and St. George. Twenty-five animals went to St. Paul Island and fifteen to St. George. The herd on St. Paul prospered. In fact, it had a population explosion. By

1938 it had 2,000 reindeer and everybody was happy. But the numbers went down faster than they went up. By 1950, there were only 81. Why? There were several reasons. The chief one seems to be that the great increase in animals had completely denuded the island of lichen—the reindeer's most important food. In addition, there was a war and for several years the inhabitants of the Pribilofs were evacuated to the mainland and the military took over. It is believed that the soldiers probably did some poaching, but the main reason for the failure of the herd must be looked for in ecological causes. The history of the reindeer on St. George Island is different, but the reasons are hard to establish. There was never such a population explosion there. The herd has fluctuated between ten and seventy-four animals, but there was never more than one deer per 100 acres. The lichens are still fairly abundant, whereas on St. Paul Island it is estimated that it may take from fifteen to twenty years for the plants to reestablish themselves.

What all this teaches us is that intensive study and research should be done before any animals are moved from their old home territory to a new environment. And in the years ahead, many dangers are looming for the reindeer-caribou and the peoples who depend on them for their livelihood. The biggest problem today is posed by the commercial development of these northern lands, especially since the discovery of oil on the shores of the Arctic Ocean.

An interesting article by Richard Corrigan in *Smithsonian* describes the first impact of the work camps on the animals of the north. Because of the instability of permafrost, which will melt if laid bare to the sun, the earlier methods of road building have been abandoned. Early roads were made by scraping off the thin layer of tundra soil and driving on the permafrost. But this resulted in deep gullies where the tires melted the permafrost. Today, roads, airfields and building foundations are all made by piling yards of gravel on top of the tundra. With the first winter, the permafrost freezes up into the roadbed, permanently stabilizing the construction. Thus, roads and airfields are usually five feet above the surrounding tundra.

The caribou have been quick to take advantage of this new situation. Plagued by mosquitoes and blackflies during the

Caribou bulls

summer, they seek higher elevations where the cool air from the sea discourages the insects. These man-made elevations supply them with welcome relief. Far from being deterred by the presence of busy workmen, they climb right up onto roadways and airfields and have proved to be a nuisance, somewhat similar to the gooney birds that have interrupted naval flights on the island of Guam. In the Arctic, when a plane is due to arrive or take off, trucks must be sent to chase the caribou from the runways, and often the men must stay there till the operation is completed, or the eager caribou will climb right back up!

The route of the controversial pipeline being built across Alaska and Canada must cross the migration routes of many caribou herds. Scientists have been experimenting with pipeline models set across the routes. These are supplied with various means of crossing for the caribou, much as fish ladders are built for salmon around dams. The pipeline is to be laid above ground much of the way, and the crossings have underpasses for the caribou to go underneath and ramps for them to go over. All but about 17 percent of the animals have refused to use either of these methods. This means that the herds will change their migration routes completely.

This has sometimes happened in the past, beginning with

the introduction of guns to the natives. As long as the animals were shot with bows and arrows, the whole herd was not alarmed. Animals were killed along the edges, but the great herd thundered on, oblivious to the danger. When guns were used, hunting was made easier for the hunter, but the noise alarmed the beasts and they associated the danger with that particular route. In a few years, they would abandon the route, and when the caribou did not turn up as expected, the human population starved.

What will happen to the people now, when the caribou refuse to cross the pipeline? And what will happen to the caribou when they can no longer reach their best food supply? Scientists are working hard to find an answer, but only time will tell. Oddly enough, the snowmobile, deplored by many conservationists, has worked in favor of the caribou. Eskimos who have taken up this machine now have fewer dogs to feed and so shoot fewer caribou.

Still another hazard threatens the northern peoples and animals—an insidious danger, also of man's making. This is radioactive fallout. The lichen plants that are the main food supply of the caribou soak up this fallout much more readily than the plants of the temperate zone. So while the fallout in the Arctic regions is really less, it is much more deadly. It has been found that Alaskan peoples that depend on reindeer-caribou meat are already contaminated with strontium 90 up to one half the permissible amount. This is a high hazard and scientists still do not know what it may mean for these northern peoples or for the caribou. Caribou and reindeer herds are much smaller than they were even a hundred years ago: an estimated 400,000 caribou and 30,000 reindeer in Alaska. And the northern human tribes are small populations. This means that if bad genes are developed because of the fallout, they will not readily be bred out of the populations. They will be inclined to increase and possibly cause the extinction of the people and creatures involved. This is another aspect of the problem which calls for careful, long-range, scientific study.

VI

THE FUTURE

14

Coming Events

These are only a few of the ecological disasters that people have brought upon themselves by moving plants and animals from one part of the globe to another to suit themselves. Have we learned anything by the experience? Are we less likely to have a new disaster to cope with in the future?

For the average person, the answer is no. Perhaps because such individuals are not aware of what has happened in the past. And today, with quick air travel that can fly us around the world in a matter of hours, it is much easier to transport plants and animals quickly and safely from place to place.

Two hundred years ago, the Hessian soldiers (so they say) brought in the destructive wheat pest, the Hessian fly, when they were stationed on Long Island during the American Revolution. Today, we have the walking catfish, brought from the Orient and released in the waters of Florida, where it is attacking the native fish. So far it has escaped all efforts to destroy it. For when a pond with such fish is poisoned, the catfish simply crawl out on land and walk away to a safer bit of water!

However, today the scientific community, and conservationists especially, are awake to the danger. Laws have been passed and quarantines established to try to keep dangerous forms of life from getting a foothold in our land. Recently, the Department of the Interior announced that it plans to make use of an old law, passed seventy-four years ago, to stop the importation of exotic animals. This law allows the department to protect the country from injurious species and it has seldom been used until now. But so great is the present flow of exotic animals from abroad, brought mainly for pet fanciers, that the department is imposing strict regulations to control it.

In 1972, two and a half million turtles, iguanas and other reptiles were brought into the country. This will be cut by 95 percent. Mammal imports will be cut by 45 percent. Birds have been quarantined for the past two years, and while the quarantine is about to be lifted, the new regulations will keep down the number of imports to about half their earlier level.

All this will be a hard blow to the pet industry, but it may save the country from some unexpected population explosion by an exotic species whose control could cost us a high price. As a side benefit, it will perhaps preserve some of these beautiful animals in their native habitats, where they are now being hunted to extinction to satisfy the pet trade in this country.

Engineers, too, are aware of the ecological dangers and now consider those aspects when planning new projects. For some years there have been studies under way for a second Atlantic-Pacific canal, for the locks of the Panama Canal cannot accommodate the new giant oil tankers. Planners study the engineering aspects and the political aspects. But today they also study the ecological problems, and that study has been responsible for the ruling out of a proposed sea-level canal.

A sea-level canal would be easier and less expensive to build, but it would also open a door between the Atlantic and Pacific oceans, so that the living creatures in both bodies of water could pass through and mingle. This could have unpredictable results, probably all bad. Fish from one ocean could attack and destroy fish from the other ocean.

One of the possible unhappy effects could be the introduction into the Atlantic of the Pacific Ocean sea snakes. Sea snakes are descended from cobras and at some period in the distant past they went back to the sea, taking with them the cobra's venom. In fact, sea snakes are many times more poisonous than cobras and are certainly something better left in their home environment. The possibility of sea snakes turning up on our sunny Caribbean beaches is not a happy thought.

And so, with scientists now aware of the dangers, perhaps our future may be more secure. But scientists, like everyone else, can become careless. And perhaps those working in the space program are less aware of the problems that we have here on earth. Perhaps that is why a satellite-tracking station, being moved from the interior of Australia to Tristan da Cunha, an island in the South Atlantic, was found to be carrying with it a colony of Australian red-backed spiders.

The bite of this spider is said to be worse than that of the black widow, and during the satellite-tracking station's journey, it stopped at a number of places, including Sydney, Australia, Honolulu and Miami. The spiders were only discovered when the equipment reached its final destination. Until that time, and the extermination of the spiders, there were innumerable opportunities for the introduction of this poisonous spider over a wide area. As far as America is concerned, I think we will all agree that the black widow is enough. But unless everyone is conditioned to think along these lines, there will always be a back door through which some unwanted pest can slip in.

Bibliography

Allen, Durward L., *Pheasants in North America*, The Stackpole Company, Harrisburg, Pa., 1956

Barnett, Anthony, "The Wild Rat," *Natural History*, November, 1959

Barnett, S. A., "Rats," *Scientific American*, July, 1967

Carr, Archie and Coleman, Patrick J., "Seafloor Spreading Theory and Odyssey of the Green Turtle," *Nature*, May 10, 1974

Chapin, James P., "Profiteers of the Busy Bee," *Natural History*, May–June, 1924

Corrigan, Richard, "Alaska Embarks on Its Biggest Boom," *Smithsonian*, October, 1974

East, Ben, "Is the Lake Trout Doomed?" *Natural History*, November 1949

Finnie, O. S., "Reindeer for the Canadian Eskimo," *Natural History*, July–August, 1931

Fuller, John G., *Fever*, Reader's Digest Press and E. P. Dutton & Co., Inc., New York, 1974

Holm, L. G. "Aquatic Weeds," *Science*, November 7, 1969

Hopf, Alice L., "From the New World—Cacti," *Garden Journal*, December, 1974

Hyams, Edward, *Animals in The Service of Man*, J. B. Lippincott Co., Philadelphia and New York, 1972

Jarvis, Woodrow, "New Weapons Against the Lamprey," *Natural History*, September, 1955

Kane, Julian, "Surtsey," *Natural History*, March, 1967

Kent, George, "The Remarkable Reindeer," *Marvels and Mysteries of Our Animal World*, Reader's Digest Assn. Inc., Pleasantville, N. Y., 1964

Kupper, Walter and Roshardt, Pia, *Cacti*, Thomas Nelson & Sons, London, 1960

Langer, William L., "The Black Death," *Scientific American*, February, 1964

Laycock, George, *The Alien Animals*, Ballantine Books, New York, 1966

Levi, Wendell M., *The Pigeon*, Levi Publishing Co., Sumter, S. C., 1941

"The Man-Hating African Honeybee," *Insect World Digest*, March–April, 1973

National Academy of Sciences, *Final Report of the Committee on the African Honey Bee*, Washington, D. C., June, 1972

Naether, Carl A., *The Book of The Pigeon*, David McKay Co., Inc., New York, 1939

Olesen, Don, "It's a Sociable Sport," *The Milwaukee Journal Insight*, August 11, 1974

Pruitt, William O., "High Radiation in Eskimos," *Audubon*, September–October, 1963

Rearden, Jim, "Caribou, Hardy Nomads of the North," *National Geographic*, December, 1974

Reilly, Edgar M., Jr., "Pigeons," *The Conservationist*, June–July, 1973

Rogers, Georgia, *The Gypsy Moth Battle Goes On*, New Jersey League of Municipalities, #A1683, Trenton, N. J.

Scheffer, Victor B., "The Rise and Fall of a Reindeer Herd," *Scientific Monthly*, December, 1951

Schorr, Burt, "U. S. Borders Are Closed," *The Wall Street Journal*, October 15, 1974

Stewart, Paul A., "Introduction of Foreign Eggs Into Nests of Starlings and House Sparrows," *Bird Banding*, July, 1970

Summers-Smith, J. D., *The House Sparrow*, Collins, London, 1963

Surtsey Research Society, *Surtsey Research Progress Reports*, Nos. IV and VI, Reykjavik, Iceland, 1968, 1972

Thorarinsson, Sigurdur, *Surtsey*, The Viking Press, New York, 1967

Tufty, Barbara, "Meet Mr. Rat," *Science News Letter*, May 11, 1963

Webster, Gary, *Codfish, Cats and Civilization*, Doubleday & Company, Inc., Garden City, N. Y., 1955

——— "The Destructive Rat," *Natural History*, January, 1957

Woldow, Norman, "Pigeon and Man," *Natural History*, January, 1972

Zeuner, F. E., *A History of Domesticated Animals*, Harper & Row, New York, 1963

Zim, Herbert S., *Homing Pigeons*, William Morrow & Company, New York, 1949

Zinsser, Hans, *Rats, Lice and History*, Little, Brown & Company, Boston, 1934

Index